A Coloured in Full Flight,

by Georgie Calverley

G000061652

A Coloured in Full Flight by Georgie Calverley

Author's note
About the book
Preface by Andres Ilves

Book one, the boy from the barracks, an introduction

Welcome to the family

Author's note

In 2004, following a minor operation, I began an online diary to combat boredom and take my mind off the post-operative numbness. After ten days of rest and many hours of typing, I emailed my scribbles to a friend. Asked if I was writing a book, I said no. An avid reader of true crime and trashy novels, the idea of penning any kind of book was ludicrous.

However, the seed was planted, so I continued writing about my past, and adding stories relating to my present situation at the time. Basically, I had no idea what I was doing, or getting myself into, and for the next thirteen years, a keyboard became my closest friend.

This had all started around 2002, when I bought a second-hand computer. My electronic skills were amateurish to say the least and typing about any stories about myself seemed like a good idea at the time. Soon my nimble fingers raced over the keyboards whenever I had a free moment. Working as a nurse at The Lister Hospital, a private institute in central London, my new toy kept me entertained. When 2004 arrived, I had a manuscript, or it looked like one to me, and after a google search, some publishers found a file to read. Naturally, they deleted it post haste, while I waited with bated breath. I got the impression they hoped I stuck to my day job.

Finally, there was a reply. Someone wrote back and praised the story and asked if I had completed the book. We exchanged a flurry of emails and I promised to finish the book in record time. There was no clear plan. I had no clear structure or idea on how to write any book. Reading was easy, so I assumed writing a novel would come naturally. How wrong I was!

I persevered and typed every day, tucked away in a tiny flat, laying down my story onto a computer drive. Using my reading skills as a writing tool, I allowed my fingertips do the talking. My recreational writing skill were an echo of my speaking style. The sentences were long and punctuation a tool delegated to the back seat. I was good at telling stories, if short funny anecdotes counted. Wrapped up in the idea of being an author, I sent most of the scribbles to friends, and waited for their feedback.

Complimented and encouraged, they spurred me on, unaware I was some budding writer, so I kept it a secret, afraid they might tease and mock me.

Years passed, and I continued to write with less enthusiasm. The publisher was patient, told me to take my time and I did. I caught the travelling bug, flitted between California, South Africa and London, while my first book, Twisted and Torn, lengthened sporadically. Along the way, I grew bolder, picked up a few tricks along the way, and not the sort you are imagining, so I adapted my story telling skills accordingly. I was on a roll.

The book, or the idea of it, was aimed at my friends and colleagues, many who knew me – or thought they did. It is natural for people to make some random assumption or theory about another person, we are only human. It seemed my physical appearance, different or peculiar social and personal mannerisms or affectations, gave strangers reason to comment, deride and verbally abuse me. I faced a constant volley of condemnation, which was most hurtful and emotionally destructive. Yet, I gave nothing away, and I hoped the book would explain the reasons why I became an object of bad and gross misinterpretation, public or private speculation.

After 13 years of much painful rewriting, proofreading, editing, friendly and professional advice, spirited motivation and encouraging feedback, it is finally time to read part of the journey I faced to become the adult I am today.

A Coloured in Full Flight; The boy from the barracks, is the new title and it follows my path from the time I was young enough to register everyone and everything around me. This is Book One, personally written for all to enjoy and share the trials and tribulations of my life until the age of 15.

My writing journey was painfully long, yet I kept going, happy that some individual eagerly awaited the final product. In 2012, I took ten months to complete the entire novel. After several reviews and proofreads, I decided to publish it in three separate instalments. The content was emotional and tough in places, and I hope A Coloured in Full Flight creates an awesome platform and runway for the next instalment.

I thank all who contributed, directly or indirectly, and many who loitered patiently, chasing me to get it done and dusted. Staying motivated was so tough over the years, second guessing a terrible demon, and I am grateful to everyone who encouraged me to continue. Eternally grateful to the new platform, social media, for allowing me meet more wonderful friends and fans along the way. Your virtual support, kind words and comments were truly a treasure and much appreciated. Thank you very much for sharing a chapter with friends and spreading the word but thank you most of all for taking the time to read the first part of my memoir.

I thank every reader from the bottom of my heart and absolute admiration and virtual hugs to those who followed the virtual and verbal journey.

Antoinette Dunn, the original fan. Thank you for planting the idea and not sure if I want to hug or choke you for starting me on this long, painful yet exciting journey. A true friend indeed.

Ryeland Gongora, I appreciate all the encouragement, guidance, help and assistance over the years. You deserve a medal for patience. Meeting you in 1998 was a blessing, and I am glad to call you a dear and close friend. You are simply wonderful.

A kind mention to Lakis Fourouklas, for telling me my story needs to be told. Best wishes with your writing.

Totally and utterly impressed beyond words with Andy Higgins, a super talented artist, for the perfect front cover. Gerald Bedeker, you are one of a kind. My mad hatter friend, thank you so much for your artistic flair and adding that final touch to my perfect cover. You two are super awesome.

This book is dedicated to a wonderful supporter who left us too soon. We do miss you and I hope you get to read the book to all the other beautiful souls and angels in Heaven.

Surena Judith Alexander or Sue as we knew her;

28/08/1963 – 21/10/2016

To a close friend, Daniel Dalais, sorry you never got the chance to read the final chapter, you will be missed by your loving family and friends;

10/10/1974 – 14/05/2018

About the book

A Coloured in Full Flight is about my painful journey sprinkled with bits of adolescent angst, many emotional teenage encounters and burdened by physical adult strife in a hard, sometimes cruel and unforgiving society.

Started as a diary, it covers much of my past and certain events, episodes and characteristics I kept hidden from friends, family and colleagues. My childhood and adolescent years were riddled with varying and sometimes constant barrage of verbal, physical and inappropriate sexual behaviours. I grew to be a quiet, shy and insecure teenager, isolated and ostracized for being different, mocked for acting like a girl. No one saw the dark halo of low self-esteem and dented self-confidence. I was adept at masking much of my internal misery.

Throughout life we meet people, some remain and become a close friend, while others move, becoming an acquaintance, a beautiful or perhaps some bad memory. Life and circumstances shape us into the adults we present to the world and those around us. My first book is about growing up poor, disadvantaged and bullied child in South Africa, during the time of much racial segregation and discrimination. Disconnected from the social issues we all faced, I felt threatened and alone, surrounded by those meant to lift and inspire me.

If you never believed in guardian angels, A Coloured in Full Flight might change your perception. I am proof they do exist.

Preface

I have had the pleasure of knowing George for the better part of a decade. Or, more to the point, I thought I knew him until I read the first part of his manuscript and gripping memoir.

How such a long history of suffering unspeakable cruelty, and at such a tender age to boot, did not lead to permanent damage to the soul, eludes me. The George I know - a dynamic, vibrant, kind and caring soul - exhibits no trace of having endured such degradation based on his race and sexual orientation in the apartheid-era South Africa.

Like the story of South Africa itself, George's narrative is one not dominated by the oppression of the past, but reflective of a deep and abiding strength of character. It is a story not of tragedy, but of triumph.

Andres Ilves

Cape Town

March 2018

Book One: The boy from the barracks

Introduction

Throughout the ages, children were conceived out of love, or that was the presumption. As we grow older, we learn there may be varying degrees of passion or pain during conception. Whatever the reason, our parents share a brief period of human interaction. Love, happiness, hate, fear, misery or joy and lust, pain, anger or hatred are some factors which could affect the bond between parents and the new baby. Every situation will be different, but the goal remains the same. Parents and loved one's expect the new arrival to be healthy and perfectly formed, praying nature would take its natural course.

Various natural and miraculous physiological cycles and hormones play a big part in foetal development over the next nine months. Nature, science, nurturing and life, or later, something called fate or destiny, may offer us a run for our money. At the mercy of the universe, the baby must depend on a group of people to raise, care and nurture it into adulthood, the warm womb would become a distant memory as parent's and child bond, before leaving the confines of the labour ward and hospital.

The stage is set, lights focused, another chapter waiting to unfold. We, as humans, sometimes predict a story line, but life comes at a price, the so-called fairy tales were never on our cards. Elders or loved ones would nod and offer guidance, nurture and protect the child, as they travelled along a meandering path called life.

The above-mentioned path, filled with copious amounts of good, bad, evil or happiness, faced one infant, me. Unaware, that most good or happy would be missing, I encountered a path speckled with many unkind and beastly human beings. No one had prepared me for it, so there I was, pure, innocent and defenseless, and I would learn how to manage, tolerate and cope with the malicious individuals. I had no idea why they I was the chosen one, singled out to be the main attraction in the ensuing story. It is my life, by the way, so who else should be the star, but I.

As we age, life has a way of dealing a healthy dose of tricks upon us. The physical, emotional and mental demands we face daily, instill a person with the capacity to adapt or adjust, to fit in, following the set rules in a society. For those who faced the cruelty or abuse, we may debate and bicker about fate being a predetermined factor. I left a safe cocoon, a warm protective amniotic sac to face a bad world, since the universe may have promised, but society had other ideas for me. It was as if someone had set out the stepping stones before my arrival.

My personal journey on the highway to infamy, misadventure and serious misfortune had begun. As a neonate, they called me a baby boy, and I had to become an infant, then a toddler and adolescent. Ridiculed as I became a teenager, my voice broke and cracked, pesky hormones plagued me, and I grew taller and bigger in stature. I was repulsed by unwanted body hairs and could not understand why. There was nothing I could do yet accept I would become what everyone expected of me, a man.

My smooth skin erupted in red angry spots. Bouts of acne dotted most of my formative years. Assured I would outgrow them, no one trusted me to be different. Blackheads, white-heads, red or yellow heads, I had them all, a part of my daily close. Would I become a working teenager or some young employable adult in the future? Society, and perhaps my parents or relatives, expected a lot from me, because I was born into a culture, and it would take a few years before the reality touched base.

There was a set standard of rules. Basic, social and parental expectations. I had to follow or face some penalty or admonishment. Good manners are a given rule, attending school another, until our grey cells peaked enough and gave up. Once out of school, the next port of call was to find a job, to pay back the parents for doing a good job in raising and caring for you. It was to be a very ordinary and normal life. If only it were true.

Born and named Georgie David Calverley, I was called David and not by my first name. A small barefoot child, I raced around a wooden shack we called home, chasing rats, playing games and pranks to pass the time. No one told me I was poor or underprivileged. Before my 6th birthday, I had a real new brick house, surrounded by soft sand, and a big oil refinery. The other kids were like me, I made new sets of friends, yet different rats. All in the name of torture, fun and frolics.

Blissfully unaware my life would take a sharp yet menacing turn, I started primary school after I turned six. Somehow, someone made time to plant an unsavoury seed before we had to pack up and leave the area. This time I would move further away, leave the big brick home and enter another, if not smaller wooden shack. Lack of a suitable living space was the least of my concerns as time passed. Remember, someone had planted a bad seed, so the person watered the unsavoury pod. Germination was slow, as well as a bit pleasurable, painful and provoking.

After some years, nine to be exact, I fought to preserve my sanity, a sense of composure and strength, as life dealt me one heavy blow after another. Shrouded in almost constant misery, I retreated to a private and personal place, vowing never to show any signs of weakness.

I started school, became Georgie to teachers and classmates, yet remained David to family and relatives. Later, I would be called many things as the other kids screamed and laughed, joining in the fun at my expense. Still a bit young to understand the depth and meaning, their words would follow me for many years, tainting my self-esteem and self-worth. Life had wired me differently. I was not like the other boys, nor did I act, behave or even think like them. Some thing or someone was playing tricks a trick on me. I was tainted and weird, teased, taunted and mocked. I remained silent, as I raced away to shed a tear in private. There was no one around me, I had to fend for myself. Once the dust had settled, the damage had been done.

Joining the girls, I avoided rough games or sports with the boys. I was the sissy, the girly one in the mix. It was a fun name at first, then the mention took on a different tone as my fame spread. No one at home said anything to me, nor did we talk me being different. I was a son, a brother, a normal boy in every way, as far as my family was concerned. Children teased me throughout the day, tunes and tones changed, as words became a recitation or mantra, when I appeared. Later, a word instilled fear and doubt, creating a shallow bed of low self-esteem and a social insecurity at a time I needed support the most. The formative years left me feeling bad about who and what they made me to be, while I merely wanted to be part of the social groups around me. They made me an outsider, and kept me a few feet away, praying and wishing to join their set.

Suitably surrounded by many kids taunting, pestering and tormenting me, no one ever said they were bullies at all. It was childish games, soon to be forgotten until the newest plaything or playmate came along. In my case, they were so very wrong.

Before I relocated, I was a girly boy to sissy, but that changed to a moffie – the derogatory term meaning sissy or queer. I was never called a friend or anything like that, and if anyone did, I was unaware of it. It was always the horrible names. David, Georgie or a sissy, I was one of three, I did not need a nickname, usually given to kids by friends, family or relatives.

I was something to be looked down upon, hated and despised for being a sissy. Associated with all things unacceptable, yet strangely, no one in the family brought up the topic or my teasing. Did they know or was better to ignore and admit to having a gay son and sibling? Their silence prompted me into a deeper isolation. It seemed no one cared how I felt or was made to feel, leaving me out on my own.

Taking the name calling on the chin, I smiled and bore it, hiding the pain. Singled out and teased, taunted and later touched inappropriately, the next dose of bullying became a long-term prescription. When I was strong and ready to fight back, the mental and emotional scars were deeply engraved into my head and heart. From age eight, throughout my schooling and the next few tertiary years, I had little or no respite from the bullies, young or old, educated and illiterate. I never fought back, silently stood my ground, and took the verbal flogging like the man I wasn't.

Along the way, a teacher suggested I become George, it should knock the sissy out of me. It didn't work. I remained a sissy, and a moffie. Accused purely on some unknown mechanism enabling me to act, feel and behave differently. Some boy started it, and others followed, I was touched, and it led to some physical contact, unsure how to react, I was conditioned into a pattern of acceptance. There was a pattern, I never fought back at all.

The next stage was a given, others followed. Rejected by many, yet there were those who needed and touched me. I was filled with mixed emotions as bullies and suitors dragged me in every direction. Loved one minute or hated the next, I had to deal with the mixed messages, giving them access to drive, lead or dictate my emotions for the day. I wanted to be loved and accepted, yet hated their actions, while society was determined in making my life a living hell. I could not be me, since it was against the rules.

As they fashioned me into a scared little boy, boxing me into an insecure teenager and young man, sending an adult into the world with a dented or low self-esteem, and lacking in social and personal confidence. Basically, I was an internal emotional mess, physically, an almost perfect specimen. Welcome to my story.

In this tale, I grow bigger, stronger and healthy as expected, while fingers pointed in my direction, the pansy and sissy in their midst. Belittled, I had no boyish brashness or bravado to fight or argue against the merciless and cruel society. Shelving my strength and energy, I stood tall and proud, the secret tucked away, even as I was publicly ridiculed. No one knew what it took to hang on to my self-respect and dignity.

Who would win this battle? Society had nothing to lose or gain, while the family expected me to make some success of my life. Born poor, I was an isolated gay child, teenager and adult. Everyone frowned upon me, except my family and relatives who remained stone-faced, never really coming a step closer or to my rescue. I walked a rocky path, climbed mountains of misery and abuse, unsure how it would all end.

Read along, see how I coped and managed. I urge you to join in this journey towards a destination of the discovery of my Truth.

Welcome to the Family

Daddy, the radio loving cow man

To understand my upbringing, and what made me who I am, let us start with my dear parents. If there were two mismatched people in my eyes, then they were those two, Uncle Nkomo and Aunt Koekoe. They were my parents, but relatives referred to my dad and mom as, Nkomo meaning 'cow' and Koekoe 'chicken,' respectively. I called them Mommy and Daddy. Although he was born Archie Berry, my father was called Tata Nkomo all his life. 'Tata' means father, for respect, and 'cow' was a pet name. How he got that name I don't know, but growing up on a farm, he was good at herding the animals, they said. Others knew him as a skilled slaughterer of livestock, be it cows, sheep or goats that were needed to feed the masses at parties, weddings or funerals.

Xhosa and Zulu were the two languages he spoke throughout his life. His command of English was decent enough but because of his native African tongue, he struggled with the Afrikaans language, which was my mother's main language of communication. The irony of this was not understood until we were older and wiser. My dad was one of 12 children, or so I am led to believe. My parents' ancestry is very hazy and mostly supposition on my part. I am very sad to think that I have so little knowledge of my own parents' early years or thereafter. Way back then, kids asked no questions and were meant to be seen rather than heard. Children were not encouraged to entertain or interfere during adult conversation, so eavesdropping became somewhat of a childish game. Information filtered down, was sifted through our little brains as we grew, while they diverted questions with suitably edited answers. That was the culture my parents were raised in and handed down to us as children.

Please do excuse the very sketchy family tree but I will try to fill the gaps as I write and scavenge for information. My dad's parents were Thomas William Calverley, who made his way from Britain to live as a settler in the Transkei, and Mariah, a local woman from the same area. According to a relative, Thomas had come from England with his wife and children, so Mariah could not have been married to the white soldier who became a farmer. Maybe Mariah had worked on his farm. Perhaps not, or he may have had a few kept women around the farm, when one took stock of the many uncles that I encountered during family reunions. There were too many variations of skin tone and physical traits among the Calverley clan.

Mariah must have been of black or coloured descent, or should I say mixed or biracial, so as not to offend some readers. I was born 'coloured,' as indicated on my birth certificate, and the title of this book will not change.

My uncles spoke Xhosa fluently, since that was the local language in most parts of the Transkei, a black homeland within the confines of South Africa. It had been set aside, with a few other areas, for a specific ethnic group, mainly the blacks. The whites living in these designated areas were generally farmers and traders, so naturally they hired the non-white residents as servants and helpers. Lust and love were sure to blossom among racial barriers, but I will not dwell on that right now.

According to a relative, Thomas had died in the Boer War. Even though Mariah is not mentioned on his death certificate, they had twelve children together. Seven of those who lived were boys, and there was one baby girl who survived childbirth. I had never seen or met this aunt or if I did, I recall none of it. Despite supposedly sharing the same parents, they all had similar facial features but not the same skin colour. My dad was a dark chocolate brown, perhaps darkened by the sun. Others were less tanned, while another was very fair and could have been mistaken for a white person.

Another was a miniature version of his taller brothers. Dwarfism, autism and mental disease was somewhere in the Calverley genes. A well-kept secret or a slip in my memory? It is normal to ask how to do the same parents produce kids with so many different traits, yet they shared familiar features? While every uncle spoke Xhosa or Zulu fluently as a first language, so did most of the women they chose to marry. Well, except for my mother, who could hardly speak nor understand the African vernacular.

I am not saying that either of my forebears might have fooled around, but one does wonder if some of the brothers were half-brothers at most. Drastic racial laws came into play well after my parents' birth. Perhaps Mariah was saddled with all the dark-skinned kids, even if one or two brothers could easily be mistaken for white. I guess no one asked any questions either over an unwed mother producing this vast array of kids with different skin tones. So, my grandmother may have been a kept woman for that matter, but we may never know the answers to that. One might think he may have dumped some of his illegitimate kids with her, leaving her to face the music alone, or she might have been no angel either.

Perhaps she raised them as siblings, despite their external features being dissimilar, though it was obvious that they shared one or both parents. That is my take but let us not speak ill of the dead and redirect the story back to my father.

Thanks to randy old Thomas, I garnered pure English genes from my dad's side of the family tree and so I got to know of uncles: John, Charles, Wellington, Alfred, George and Percy to name a few. We shall stick to Uncle Nkomo, my father and a man no one ever called by his birth name, Archie Berry.

He was born on 30 September 1927, on a farm located in the black homeland of Transkei, called Ngqeleni. Richard Calverley was the original British settler to set foot on African soil, so we thank him for planting his seed which created our clan of mixed race people, with the help of his son Thomas, whose family, like many other 1820 British colonists, were shipped by the British government to the

South African Eastern Cape region to create or start a new life, not to mention their mixed-race offspring. Most of them would be shunned later when the country decided to be tough on its non-white residents with the infamous Immorality Act

My dad's facial features were almost like that of his wife and soul mate. Both had high cheekbones, but his pitch-black eyes and dark brown skin were a strong contrast to my mother's fair complexion and bright green eyes. My dad was lean, tall and wiry all his life, and walked around using a self-styled wooden walking stick. He had a permanent hunched-over gait and always complained of a stiff and painful back. With a semi-balding head covered with sparse thin black and grey hair, he loved nothing more than sitting in his vegetable patch, reading the horse-racing page and smoking his pipe filled with tobacco. The other 'crushed leaves' I would know about at a later stage in life.

Archie was very much a loner, a taciturn man as he ambled around bent over his shiny walking stick. He took pride in polishing the wooden clubs or sticks or making new 'knobkerries' for others – a word derived from the Afrikaans word knop, meaning ball or knot, and kerrie, which is a cane or walking stick. Sometimes this ornate stick was used as a weapon to fend off dogs and unruly people alike.

He was good at using a knife on wood. There was some vague explanation that he had injured his back during the war or while working in the mines, thus rendering him unable to work. The government paid him a meagre monthly disability pension to care for himself and later for a wife and three kids. My father never worked at a paying job for as long as I recall, so he had a daily routine which included using his walking stick to prod and poke in the sand or dirt as he went on his merry way, something a farmhand or herder would do. Anything and everything had to be investigated for possible use around the house or farm.

Schooling and education was something he considered a good thing for his kids, but so did everyone. It was drummed into our heads from an early age. I found out that both my parents had little or no schooling. They were illiterate and could just about read, write, sign their name, or understand basic English. This did not affect how they raised us, expecting respectful, good mannered and well-behaved children towards relatives and strangers alike.

For someone who was uneducated, my dad had lots of worldly social knowledge that he would lecture us on. The 'psychology' of things was his favourite word and only now do I wonder if he knew what it really meant. From his point of view, family was first, and being nice to strangers in case "you too might need a favour one day" was a common lecture. "Be nice until they prove you wrong," he said, so it was important for us to learn from our elders, as they had been kids once many moons ago.

Respect went a long way, I was told, but education was the key to making a better life for oneself. At the time I had no idea what he meant, but adult conversations rarely stuck in our brains until it was too late. Parents, illiterate or not, usually expected and wanted the best for their kids. Mine were no different in that respect. They would raise us to be God-fearing citizens, well-behaved and polite, while the rest was left for me to fathom or fight alone.

Lack of schooling did not hamper my father's love for gardening or growing vegetables to sell or feed us in times of need. All my siblings, and others, pitched in to help create the space and plant and water it for him. He would sit on his makeshift stool and dish out orders as we ran off to give, deliver and bring back the payment. Not everyone paid and sometimes there was no money, but he still gave in the hope that they would cough up later when we needed a favour. Poverty made friends among many yet also created some enemies.

My helpful father gave, they ate, and we would end up begging for the payment most of the time. He would often intervene just as our game with friends heated up, calling on us to run an errand or two. We knew how far to push him until the tone of his voice changed, forcing us to get a move on and deliver the vegetables. Sometimes it was tough when no money was handed over and he would look crestfallen, especially when things became a bit too tight or sparse on our own table. There were only so many vegetables, raw or cooked, one could eat.

He put so much work into his garden. While we hated helping, that was no issue, and we enjoyed whatever the garden produced. Expecting us to be at his beck and call to deliver, we knew how to run, hide or delay until he spoke his native Xhosa. That is when we knew it was time to quit. My father hardly ever raised his voice unless pushed too far by his naughty offspring. While we understood him, we always responded in English. We couldn't speak his native languages despite brave efforts to teach us along the way. If we understood him, that was fine and dandy. With games to play, we became bored with a few tongue twisting click sounds, racing away to annoy or impress friends with a new word.

Other than the work in his garden, selling vegetables and visiting his brothers, he was not a very active person. He loved listening to the radio, especially the drama stories they read over the airwaves. Sitting quietly in front of his little transistor radio promptly at 8 p.m. for his favourite serial, no one would disturb him or make a noise. Performed in Xhosa or Zulu, we sometimes listened to his interpretation, as he explained along the way or during a break. It was scary and exciting, but there was always a message to learn from these stories, we knew. I am that sure he made them up as he went along, but we enjoyed them since there was no television around to keep us entertained. My father's dramatic storytelling did the trick as we huddled together in the semi-darkness.

Using candles or small fires burning in a cutout metal drum, the emotive voices and eerie music on the radio created tension in the air. Scared to move as our shadows sometimes scared us, it made sleeping difficult at times. We had to stay till the end of the story and would be back the next night. That I am neither a horror movie fanatic nor a television fan might have something to do with this period of my life.

After his garden and radio stories, spending time and wasting money on horse racing was his other great pastime. My mother hated the latter since we saw no spoils, or not that we knew of, so it was just money dished down the drain, she moaned. Not bothered about wasting money, he sometimes made a trip to a nearby racecourse, taking us for a day out. I loved the excitement as the voice on the loudspeaker shouted out names and numbers with people jostling and shouting over one another. My father seemed to soak up the atmosphere, not too bothered if he never won anything. He looked happy and relaxed away from his garden and we had to face my mother when we returned a few hours later.

Like most kids, we grew bored after a while, wandering around the stands, eyes cast down looking for fallen coins or anything of value, the curse of a child who never had pocket money. Between races, I joined other kids as we raced around on all fours, pretending we were horses. Of course, I was the fastest. We never got too close, but I liked the look and magnificence of the horses as they preened before the race. The tiny brightly-coloured jockeys looked relaxed until they hung on for dear life during the race as we screamed for our favourite. Dirty, poor and happy, we straggled home until next time.

My love for horses grew steadily, despite being very scared of the beautiful beasts. It took many years before I summed up enough courage to attend a horse-riding lesson. Being the oldest, insecure student who had only ever watched horses from afar, I ignored all the giggles around me. Kids who spent all their little lives feeding, grooming or riding were going to find me funny astride a sedated horse. My horse was a rebel, going out of the circle as I kept my panic in check and let the teachers rein him in. I did not want to be too harsh or pull too hard on the reins; my fat ass on his back was painful enough. We looked an odd pair and three lessons later, we all knew I was never going to race off into the sunset with the wind in my hair. One box on my bucket list had been ticked off as we side-stepped the story.

Once a month, my father would dress up neatly to go into town to collect his government disability pension. Wearing well-worn formal pants and a shirt and suit jacket, he looked very different to the man who sat among his growing vegetables. Usually, his outfit was not colour-matched, but they were clean and presentable with a tie being optional. One did not want to look too formal either, since you were looked down upon anyway as you waited in line. Payments were not always on the same date of every month nor were you guaranteed payment on arrival, and families had to beg or borrow amongst one another until they received the paltry pension.

After he gave my mother his share towards the household upkeep, she let him indulge in his once a month delicacy of tripe, edible lining from farm animals, especially cow, sheep, goat and for the kids, chicken. Cooked, of course. Rounded up to clean bits of whatever he came home with as we heaved at the smell and consistencies. Once cooking began, the smell drove everyone out of the house.

My mother hated it and made a point of visiting some of her family members once cooking was under way. Once cooked, we had no issue eating the tripe at all. My mother refused point blank, and if tripe was not available, my father came home with a bag of ox livers. Same story and scenario, mother fleeing the house as we waited for the meat to cook and enjoy. We ate very well afterwards, thank you. No complaints at all to the chef. Food was food to us, meat did not come our way very often, unless at a party, wedding or funeral. Even then you had to fight for your piece.

Grant day was nice because we went into the town to replenish food supplies. Town as a child to me was merely a small group of Indian-owned shops that sold basic food and household utensils. The real big town was too far and a car ride away, a luxury no one around us could afford.

Generally, on grant day we ate all things sweet, tasty or forbidden on other days. Kids begged for money to buy more sweets, to impress or buy friendships. Frazzled or annoyed parents were circled until they gave in and flung money our way. Friends lasted if the money got them sweets before deserting you for another golden goose. Your time in the spotlight was short-lived, and I assumed most, or every parent got a grant from the government.

Sadly, as kids we only wanted to be good at being children and not too bothered over the mechanisms of being a good one. There would be time for that later, yet sadly I wished I had paid more attention to my father's ramblings and asked more questions. I could have learned so much from this quiet, unassuming and mild-mannered man. If only I had taken the time to do so then, when he had all the time and patience in the world to pass on facts about his family and my ancestors. Sadly, I never made time for him, even when we both needed it the most, until we realized that it was too late on so many levels.

My father was a true man of the earth, who lived a plain and simple life with all that was available to him, and never appeared to be fazed with what was going on around him. He was most happy surrounded by the brush, leaves, trees, vegetables and his radio as he sat quietly watching the world go by. We all knew where to find him, and I often wondered what he thought about as he smoked his pipe and gazed through the smoke.

mommy, the shy green-eyed griqua

My mother was born Elizabeth Kok in Mount Frere, which was also in the Transkei. Her parents were Martha and Atoor Kok, and there were four sisters and two brothers in the family. She was very secretive about her birth, which was on 18 February 1931.

Afrikaans was her mother tongue, and she could speak no Xhosa or Zulu, or have any conversation with her husband in these languages. My father could speak no Afrikaans either, so one wonders how the hell did they court each other. Their English was basic at best, so we had four different languages floating around us at one time or another. I veered towards English, while my older siblings chose Afrikaans. No one spoke back to my dad in his native tongue, but we understood him very well. How strange it may sound, but there was very little miscommunication among the five of us. Like other homes around us, this was very much the norm indeed.

My mother was quiet, shy, reserved, and a housewife all her life, and like my father, a monthly grant came her way. Other than suffering from asthma, no reason was given for her unemployed status or whether she ever had a job before we, her children, came along. She lived to keep her house neat and tidy, no matter where we lived. Like all farm-raised kids, she woke at dawn, irrespective of the day or season. We needed no alarm clock, and there was never a time to have a few extra minutes under the covers unless you were sick. Only sick people had to be in a bed when the sun was up. We saw no need to hurry out of a warm bed if there was no school or work to attend. Beware if you had an appointment the next day: my dear mother woke before the cock crowed to hen peck you out the door. She was also a natural worrier over anything and everything, compared to her very laid-back husband. They were very different in many ways, and we saw nothing wrong with this picture as they were our parents.

The housework was done early in case we had any visitors, so the place had to be shiny and tidy. In the rural setting where my mother was raised, women rose early to prepare the household for the day. This trait was thus ingrained as much as her kids hated it. When the sun shone bright and early, laundry had to be done and dried before any signs of rain or dark clouds. She cooked and prepared the evening meal at the earliest convenience. Whether we access to electricity or not, things were no different as she cooked or cleaned in case of mishaps or unanticipated surprises. There were no impromptu meals for us and everything was planned the day before or very early in the morning and she took great pride in her home and making sure we were fed and comfortable.

A homely and private person, she rarely ventured out unless it was necessary, and her usual outings were to church on Sundays, the hospital or clinic due to her asthma, or to collect her disability grant. With little money, she only used one occasion to visit relatives on both sides of her family. My mother and sister did most of the visiting while my dad only went if there was a need or he was summoned for an elders meeting. My brother and I were left to our own devices, but I tagged along with my mother when I could. I knew there would be food, drinks or sweets offered.

An illness, death or birth in the family, a birthday, wedding celebration or some other relative-oriented issue made us leave our home together as a family unit. Other than that, we kept a low profile in the neighbourhood and were a very private family.

Looking back, we had very few visitors to our home, unless as mentioned above, and I never wondered why. There was never a DO NOT VISIT US sign outside our house, so the nice crockery reserved for visitors was seldom used from the display cabinet in the dining room. We were not an unfriendly bunch either, so it was strange that people gave our house and home such a wide berth. Even as an adult, I found it very hard to allow anyone into my own personal private living space, I still do, and made the effort to go out and visit closest friends at their homes instead. Maybe I might hit on the reason or find an answer to this odd mannerism as I write along.

When it came to anything related to our schooling, over time, we excused our parents with some lame reason why they could not attend a meeting or function. Sickness or ill health was a usual one, but I am sure the teachers knew why many parents avoided the school unless it was very necessary. If we behaved, there was no need for a teacher to demand that a parent drop in. Some brought an uncle or aunt when push came to shove. My parents were happy to sign any document or let my elder siblings do so on their behalf. My mother, like my dad, was there to care for and feed us, and despite our family ties, I never felt a close mother and son bond, or father and son bond either, but it was not something that left any impression until I began to write this book.

My mother suffered from asthma and during our rainy winter months, her visits to the clinic or hospital increased, and it was painful to watch her suffer. A very independent woman, she reached out to her sisters and family when things got tough yet remained stubborn to a fault. Calling an ambulance was a hassle and she hated people fussing over her, never mind that she had a problem with her breathing.

Keeping her clinic visits was as important as her regular Sunday church attendance. The Methodist church saw her every weekend, wearing pretty one or two-piece outfits, and she never left for church without a hat. Only her asthma attacks, bad weather, or lack of bus fare were reasons for missing a church service. It was important to pay her tithes, despite our needing the money more. We had no idea how much she put into the neat white envelope, but I enjoyed tossing it into the round brown dish passed along the pews. She felt bad if there was nothing to offer, while my father had no interest in setting a foot through the door of God's house.

As the keeper of the home, it was her responsibility to buy clothes for us kids, but there was no spur of the moment shopping sprees. Planned weeks or sometimes months in advance, our clothes were 'lay-byed,' which meant a down payment on items chosen until the full amount was paid. We collected the new clothes even if they were out of fashion by the time we got to wear them. Feeling ecstatic about having new stuff to wear, one gave little thought to fashion sense at the time, prancing and preening amid a mixed bunch of impressed or jealous kids.

The other kids could not ruin the clothes, but they could sure stamp their dirty feet on your new shoes. It was a new shoe initiation as far back as I could recall. Some kids avoided the shoe stomping by making new shoes look worn and dirty. School shoes had to be polished every day, which was a sign of good parenting skills, but it did give our shoes a longer life.

Given that we depended on financial handouts from the government and relatives, we lived from day to day as most people in our neighbourhood did. The Calverley home, with very basic furniture, ornaments and household goods, was kept clean and orderly. My mother the farm girl took pride in any place we called home, and she seemed happiest and comfortable around her own things.

Everything had to be cleaned and polished to it former shining glory. Brasso, a metal polish, used to shine the cheap silver, brass and other metals. Every home had a furniture, floor or ornament rag at hand to mop, shine and clean. Kids had to help wherever and whenever they were called upon. You could grumble and drag your feet but there would be no escape. As we grew older, all that changed.

Of all the ornaments we owned over the years, the porcelain dogs and fish one could put potted plants in were the ultimate vulgarity. Yet every household had to own one or many, and they came in pastel shades of pink, blue or green or some bright hideous colour. Hateful stuff! Oh, and not to forget the hanging mirrors shaped like birds or butterflies, with small bright pieces of broken glass around the edges. Then there were the pictures made of cloth, picking up dust over time; they call it embroidery today. Back then, it was what made every house a home.

Most households were judged on flashy wallpaper glued onto wooden or brick walls, usually changed close to Christmas time as we tried to impress with the latest flowery pattern. This was accompanied by a matching linoleum on the floor. Carpets were never seen or laid out in any house that we lived in. My mother hated dust and carpets were tough to wash or clean, while linoleum only needed polish and elbow grease. The floral printed wallpaper, matching lino, and strategically placed garish ornaments were the common decor in any home. This gave a lot away when it came to style and class. Being poor did not mean you had no style or taste, but if it filled a gap and looked nice, we never refused any gifts or hand-me-down accessories. My mother was one for matching colours and keeping things in a tidy and orderly fashion. Nothing had to stand or be out of place in the home.

She and my father would argue over the radio, as she also loved her Afrikaans stories. Batteries had to be saved, he argued, if anyone wanted to listen to anything. He would sit in the garden and she stayed inside the house, both sometimes appeared to be daydreaming. During the first years of my life, there was no television, one radio between us, and very few newspapers or magazines to read, so I try now to fathom why my parents spent time apart and what they thought about, cloaked in their peaceful serenity.

Jumping ahead and many years later, when we did afford a television set, my mother could be found staring at the screen, watching soap operas. The Bold and Beautiful or Days of our Lives characters seemed very real to her and my sister. They discussed in detail all the actors' shenanigans as if they lived around the corner, never missing an episode. She could hardly wait for the time to arrive as she settled down and asked us to switch on the television set, scared she might press the wrong button. Once settled, there would be no moving about or talking to distract them from watching the virtual drama unfold. My dad once again had no interest in television unless it had horses running on it. I had the simplest parents and yet I had no idea who they really were, and I find that so sad.

I grew up in an era when kids did not ask impertinent or probing questions, which is just as sad when I think of all the wonderful history I might have picked up and how these two strange individuals became my parents. They produced three very different siblings and, as you will find out, the apples did not fall very far from the parental tree at all. It may be hard to accept and acknowledge that I may have failed as a brother or a son but let me finish the story before you decide or judgement.

A natural worrier, a trait I might have inherited from her, she agonized over us as we began to spread our wings. Another mini detour to the future to explain how my elder siblings created problems when they became teenagers and young adults: our mother would not settle until they came home, making sure they were in bed. If not, she kept an all-night vigil when no one appeared. This annoyed me very much as I expand later in the book. I was not their mother, nor did I have any understanding of the maternal instinct.

My kind, soft-spoken, caring, loving, parents, were everything a child could expect or ask for, and they instilled the basic values within me to grow, function and socialize as an adult. Despite lacking in social credits and skills, they showed me how to decipher right from wrong and the good from the bad. Those basic life skills, that no money or common sense could buy, I understood from an early age. A good standard of respect and good manners for others and myself have carried me this far in life.

Sadly, I never truly appreciated my parents, and as I grew older, I found it even harder to adjust to living with people whom I knew so little about and vice versa. It felt as if I led two separate lives at the same time. There was the humdrum of family life among my siblings and parents, and a segregated existence I maintained away from them among friends, relatives and strangers.

I would grow up shy and insecure about what I called my home, but also felt socially insecure for having illiterate parents, though most households had a similar status. I was a good child, but never the model son and young adult, during the time my mum and dad were around. It is embarrassing to admit that I fell short, and sadly there is no way to make up for that. All I can do is ask for her forgiveness, and keep in mind that she never stopped loving me, even when I was at my most disobedient and distant. It is too late to show them all my appreciation for everything they did for us, and I pray they are looking down at me from heaven and smiling at the good person I have become despite all the battles and hardship we all faced.

Rosie and Frank Boy

My sister Rosie was born on 9 December 1961, named after her plump rosy cheeks. She was fair-skinned and pretty. My brother Frank Boy was born in June 1964, on date unknown to me – or I may have just forgotten. Brown-eyed with black hair, he grew up to be wiry and lean like his dad. He was a quiet, reserved, and intelligent boy who grew up to love soccer, comic story books, and cowboy and karate movies. Boy, as we all knew him, made choices in his young life to fill an immediate need as some teenagers do. He was a loner, like the solitary cowboys and dangerous men in the novels he read. He never seemed to be in a hurry, slinking around the house and hardly speaking. One got the impression that he was impatient when he spoke, and even though we lived under the same roof, he was a total stranger to me. Like my mother and father, my brother would live to remain a mystery to me. Now you may be wondering if it really is possible for me to know little or nothing about those closest to me. Regretfully it is very much the truth.

That was my immediate and closest family, and anyway, none of us kids were blessed with my mother's stunning green eyes. Bummer! It would have made my life so much easier growing up, I would say, as the importance of this may be detailed somewhere down the line.

Our older brother, Leonard

Leonard, my half-brother, was born to my dad and a lady called Sarah. He didn't live with us but passed through our lives sporadically. I don't know if my dad and Sarah were married. We never knew of her until much later, nor did I ever lay eyes on her. Did my father leave her for my mother, or had they broken up before he met his green-eyed wife to be? I may never know the answers. Leonard was a transient soul and like his mother, we knew little of him but welcomed his short visits. After a few days or weeks, he would be gone, with no explanations given or questions asked.

Me, myself and I

I think I am funny, friendly, bubbly, outgoing, confident and caring, yet inside exists an insecure, shy, and sometimes scared child. My personal, social, and private life did seem like an open book to many friends and acquaintances I made along my journey through life, but you will see how closed I was to them and perhaps even to myself.

As we age, people learn to edit sad stories and episodes to soften the pain, avoiding a sympathetic or apathetic overture. Sometimes I shrugged off the extent of past events or skimmed over the deep-seated pain and anguish I had to live with. Perhaps things were not that bad. You can decide. Without trying to label myself as a meek victim, I had to write it all down in the hope that I have progressed to overcome and find whatever destiny had in store for me. The truth might be painful, and we know it always hurts.

Once, I felt blessed with a complete family. Sadly, as time passed, one by one, those I loved most were taken, far beyond my reach. Today, I live with no reasoning or explanation as to why these painful events happened to my loved ones or me. The notion that there is always a reason behind every painful experience in our lives makes me want to live a full and happy life, irrespective of my past.

Chapter 1: the nineteen-sixties, before and after, the very mention of a coloured family

I was born Georgie David Calverley, on 29 September 1967, at Addington Hospital in Durban. The hospital had been established in 1879, on the Natal South Coast of South Africa. Natal is the Portuguese word for Christmas and was founded by Vasco da Gama in 1497 as he sailed in search of a sea route from Europe to India. The main city Durban, founded in 1835, is named after Sir Benjamin d'Urban, a Governor of the Cape Colony at the time.

My birth details are sketchy at best. It was not a topic discussed with my parents, but I think the word "premature" was mentioned fleetingly. However, I have no verification of this.

For astrology fans, my star sign is Libra, apparently the masculine, positive and extroverted sign -- an "air sign." What, essentially is a Libran? Well, here is a definition that I particularly like: someone who can cooperate, persuade, mediate, reconcile or balance with a need to socialize, teach, advise, guide and harmonize associations. We are meant to be social butterflies with a special aura of harmony that attracts others.

That said, are our lives, loves, actions, emotions, dreams, and destinies really ruled by some unseen force beyond our comprehension? Would my life follow a plan, or could it have played out any differently, despite my actions, past or present? The position of the galaxy at the time that I took my first breath may have had its wires in a twist, I might say. The reality of my life was anything but harmonious or balanced.

I was born with brown eyes; unblemished, light tanned skin; ten toes and fingers (the standard allotment); deep, sunken eyes; a protruding thick top lip and with my parents' cheekbones. A head of curly black hair would follow, and one might say I was a mini carbon copy of a little Griqua baby, the tribe on my mother's side of the family.

The Griquas were a sub-group of South Africa's heterogeneous and multi-racial clan, with a unique origin in the early history of the Cape Colony, living as semi-nomadic commandos of mounted gunmen. Like the Boers, Griquas migrated inland from the Cape and established states in what are now South Africa and Namibia. The Boers were the Dutch, German and French descendants of South African settlers. Today they are called Afrikaners.

The Griquas are a racially and culturally mixed people from inter-marriages or sexual relationships between European colonists in the Cape and the Khoikhoi, said to be from around the 17th and 18th centuries. The Khoikhoi, meaning "real people," are related to the Bushmen, who trekked from Angola, Zimbabwe, Botswana, Lesotho, Namibia, Zambia and South Africa.

Adam Kok I, christened Adam Eta, was a cook who later became a slave to the Governor – in exchange for a piece of land – by his original owner and renamed Adam Kok. Imprisoned when a new Governor came along with his own cook, he was set free with gifts including a wagon, guns, gunpowder, ten oxen, and a house in Bushman's Kloof, near the Cederberg Mountains. The area is now home to the luxury five-star Bushman's Kloof Wilderness Reserve and Retreat.

After being called "bastards" by their owners, the clan became known as the Griquas. The word bastard "did not sit right on the tongue," it seemed. Many years later, they were called Coloured by the White ruling forces in South Africa when the apartheid system was born. My grandfather, Atoor Kok, emerged from this crazy bunch of mixed breeds with such an interesting and colourful past.

On my dad's side, I was lucky to be labelled a 'Pondo.' The amaMpondo were a group of black people who migrated from areas around the Great Lakes of Africa into South Africa. Some set up homes in Malawi and Swaziland while others created their own Pondoland in the Eastern Cape Province of South Africa.

I will not bore you with the factions, rifts and fights among various tribes who spoke a mixture of languages including the two my dad knew and spoke so well, Xhosa and Zulu. When Xhosa became a school subject, the clan identified with the language and are now known as the amaXhosa. The mother tongue of the Pondos, Xhosa, is one of the eleven official languages of the new South Africa.

The others are Zulu, Venda, Sotho, Tswana, Tsonga, Swazi, Northern Sotho, Ndebele, English and Afrikaans. Dutch and English were the first official languages of South Africa from 1910 until 1925, when Afrikaans was added. Dutch petered out, making English and Afrikaans the only two official languages in the country. This would last for a few years amid struggles and strife for equality between white and non-white citizens but let us get back to my ancestors.

The British annexed the Pondo people's territory peacefully to the Cape Colony in 1884. Later, from 1960 to 1962, the Pondo Revolt raged against the Bantu Authorities Act, which was part of the Apartheid legislation. They wanted various black ethnic groups moved to a "Bantu homeland," thus creating an autonomous nation. The homelands created for the blacks were Venda, Ciskei, Bophuthatswana, and Transkei, puppet states kept in line and controlled by South Africa. Transkei housed most of the Pondo people at the time, and my dad was born in one of its tiny villages.

So as a Durbanite, born with Dutch, Griqua, English, and Pondo blood in my veins, I was registered as 'coloured' on my birth certificate. Wow, I had collected many labels at an early age with no idea if they would be an asset or a hindrance. Let us find out.

Chapter 2: my childhood detour into ngqeleni: a serene holiday playground

The youngest Calverley son was born to become a man in a society and culture that prided themselves on raising men to be hardworking, good providers who care for their families and loved ones. Getting to see where my dad grew up was one of the best times of my life, before everything changed around us. Welcome to the homeland known as Transkei as we take a detour and find out how my dad got his nickname.

Ngqeleni – my dad's birthplace – was a tiny rural farm, situated among the grassy hills of the Transkei. The locals lived in mud huts, or rondavels, as roaming sheep, cows, pig's goats, chickens, ducks, geese, donkeys and horses dotted the scenery. Grass and farm land stretched for miles around the huts. Some animals were used as a workforce, while others were added to the cooking pot. On our yearly visits, it was exciting to see a new batch of baby farm animals, replacing those sold or eaten. The life of a farm animal was perilous indeed.

Until I was about twelve years old, we visited the farm every year around Christmas, to get reacquainted with relatives who lived in different cities and towns. There was the Durban clan, those already in the Transkei, and others from the East London area of Eastern Cape. Apparently, the whole of Transkei was one big extended family, since everyone seemed related one way or another. Perhaps it was merely a joke, but most people shared an uncle, aunt or cousin.

The farm was inhabited by local black or African people from the Pondo tribe, while a few white or mixed-race farmers were scattered around the place, usually closer to the main town, Umtata. There was no electricity, hardly any running water, and no street lights to guide the occasional car along the sandy roads through the area and into the distant mountains and green valley's surrounding us.

Living and moving around in the semi-darkness was not alien to me, but farm terrain was new. Ditched and grassy slopes provided many a mishap at night. Never mind the animal droppings that sent us sprawling and covered in shit. Not every animal on the farm took kindly to the city kids, and some tried to chase, kick or bite us. We were a bit annoying, I guess, but life here was simple, plain and laid back. We had to provide our own entertainment to brighten up the long hot sunny holidays.

It was a playground haven for a small inquisitive child. We followed the farm workers around the place, herding and feeding the animals every morning and evening while learning what made the locals tick. There was not much to do here; we assisted with anything that looked exciting, especially concerning the baby animals. Flitting away and hiding close to their dams, no amount of enticement with food got them closer. Their mothers kept a close eye on us if we got too close for comfort.

Many of the villagers had never been away from the farm or to a city as they worked so hard to maintain a life in this isolated place which saw one or two cars pass by in a day. We made friends and played with the local kids, who seemed surprised that we knew a few words and understood everything they said. Play and games were adjusted to suit all and sundry, and adults were called to clarify any misunderstanding. Everyone got on with each other during our short visits.

Other than animal farming, there were many fruit and vegetable crops as well, some for self-use and the rest sent to nearby villages for sale and bartering. We ate as much as we could, were treated like royalty and were spoilt rotten, to be honest. The city kids had free rein of the place, with some boundaries naturally.

There was a resident chief, who ruled or oversaw the smooth running of the village. An elder appointed by his people, he shared his knowledge and wisdom, and sorted out any social or personal problems among his subjects. Everyone was so open and friendly, I could not see what would upset them in this quiet natural setting. The old chief was a man who commanded great respect and awe from everyone. Disobeying him was not an option as his word was gospel. Locals and visitors alike had to abide by his rules.

Within this close-knit community, we never locked doors, but shut them to prevent the animals from entering and scrounging for food. The pigs were the worst, as they kept vigil at the door, snorting and trying to force their way in at any opportunity, their little piglets screeching as we chased them around the huts. All baby animals are so cute, and one shuddered to think they would end up as a meal the next time we visited.

It was high summer during our stay, and the mud huts with the thatched, wooden or tinned roofs became like a sauna. Everyone sat under trees, and used sheets or blankets pegged to branches or fences as makeshift umbrellas. The animals assumed there would be food if ever a group of people gathered in one place, often interrupting social chatter as we sought cooling in the shade.

At night, they would butt at the hut doors to get in, and our parents woke up to shout at them as if they understood, as we giggled in the dark. With straw rooftops, all open flames and lamps were put out, leaving us in pitch darkness, as the stars and the moon provided minimal lighting.

Nothing we did around the farm felt like a chore, considering we hated doing similar things back home. We happily stopped a game to run an errand on the farm, and there was no rush in the almost peaceful silence. Voices shouted orders and loud chatter filled the air, amid laughter, screaming kids, huffing, snorting and baying animals.

The radios were used sparingly for lack of reception and to save batteries. With not a single shop for miles, we came fully stocked with no intention of retracing our steps until we left. Naturally, there was no shortage of storytellers around the place, and if a radio was unavailable, we sat around listening to fictitious or real-life stories. At night it was no different, except for the dying embers of coal glowing in the drum which gave us a bit of light or warmth.

At bedtime, we fought over who would throw water into the drum to hear the hissing of the coals. The winner showed off by taking his time as the losers stared jealously. Spitefully, we hurled sand into the fire to burst his burning bubble, which often led to a scuffle in the dark. We were kids, after all. Water was collected in containers from a tiny creek close by, and it was testing, trying to navigate back to the hut with a full container of water. The villagers had a knack for carrying the buckets on their heads with ease. We tried, but with little success. The water was boiled before consumption to kill any waterborne diseases. There were also large drums placed around the huts to collect rainwater running from drainpipes.

There was work, general play and then we took a ride to the nearby coast for a fishing expedition. High sloping grassy hills were ideal for racing up and down to explore in absolute peace as fresh sea air carried our voices over the slopes. Finding a spot to be alone, I let my mind wander and daydreamed until I heard my name being called for the trip back to the farm. The dusty dirt road made the trip even more worthwhile as the car bounced along trying to avoid huge potholes or muddy ditches when it rained. My love for isolation, hills and quiet beaches had to have been nurtured around this time.

Everyone used the holiday for bartering and supplying the local villagers with our old or used clothes and materials for the home or farm. With few or no cars in the place, a donkey cart could only carry so much. We left unwanted or old clothes, shoes, toys, games, books for the villagers. They offered stuff we might need for the city to use in the gardens or home. My family had nothing to leave behind since we were poor, and I hardly had decent clothing.

We had many fruit trees around our home in the city, but the fruit on the farm looked and tasted even better. The only problem was that we ate everything in sight, not caring whether it was ripe or not. Ignoring adult advice, we knew there would be payment later. Eat now and pay later was fine as we stuffed our little tummies.

Holiday ended, the long drive home was just as fun. I missed running water and a good dose of some proper lighting. Each year, as we drove to and from the farm, we begged the adults for bread and butter to make our own sandwiches for the road. Padkos, or road food, translated directly from Afrikaans to English. A square piece of Erica butter was smeared onto the bread before any leftover meat or chips, crisps or fries were added. Wrapping all this in a clean plastic bag, we knelt on the sandwich until the butter melted to create a mushy piece of bread. Our parents were not fans of our ritual.

Days later, we complained of bloated tummies and no bowel movement, only to be reminded of eating large amounts of green fruit. Parents dug out the vilest of liquids to sort us out, castor oil or Epsom salts being the laxatives of choice for the poverty-stricken masses, given with a great big chunk of chocolate laxative known as Brooklax. Nothing tasted nice going down, and this created problems as the race for the toilet began. More about the toilet drama later, but every year we repeated the process and faced those laxatives with a sad heart and quivering tummy. Kids in the 70's sure did live for the moment.

Something my father looked forward to being holidaying in Ngqeleni every year, while my mother hated the long car trip and the cramped huts. For someone from a farm, it was not her favourite destination. Not one to have her private space invaded, we left her in the city as she no doubt worried about us. Most of us slept on foam mattresses or we begged to sleep at a new friend's place, rushing back early the next morning.

These joyful visits depended on space and transport provided to those who had none. A missed holiday on the farm meant we had to wait another year to meet any new kids or new arrivals to the family and clan.

Whether time spent in this remote village with its green hills, unspoiled ocean, and very friendly people played a role in my adult preference for leading my present single and nomadic life is debatable. I prefer my solitude, privacy and own company very much – not quite the galactic extroverted Libran.

Chapter 3: the nineteen-seventies and a big shack I called home

As far back as I can recall, from about the age of five or six, we lived in a house built from asbestos, corrugated sheet metal or "zinc" plates and wood, all from different shades, either painted or in their original condition. Each window, door or wall in the makeshift house had a different colour or texture. Everyone around us called a similarly-built shack home. Whether ours was newly built or recently vacated is a mystery to me. It was, however, the first place of abode I remember. This would have been around 1972 or so.

New shacks were erected, and everyone was involved in the process, and kids helped or hindered the workers. The noise from the hammering and chatter started early as loud music blared from the radios, and the men worked till way after sunset. Some men slept in the semi-built shacks to guard supplies and their workmanship from vandalism and nosy kids. How and when we moved into the shack is a mystery. Where did we come from in the first place? All I was told was that my parents had come here with the promise of a house in the city. So where were we living before this, I wonder.

Many unanswered questions cropped up. Did we move from a house to a shack or from shack to shack, since my parents did not work? If so, where from? Apparently, my dad was living in Cape Town, either working or looking for work. Was he already married to my mother, and if so, where were we residing in his absence? If I was born in 1967 in Durban, we must have already been living here, or close by, as I doubt a family of five would have crisscrossed the country from pillar to post, with little or no funds and transport.

Many other questions arose, and sadly there were no answers to any of them.

We started life as a family, me being the youngest of five people living in the shack. A tarred straight road ran past our front door, and beyond that was a patch of short trees, grass, weeds, and bush. Our yard had areas of soft and hard red sand and one felt like it was sea sand under your feet. In summer, the sand was as hot as hell, so we wore flip-flops most of the time. On rainy days, we played "slip and slide" as the sand turned to mud. We had to make sure no muddy trails led back into the shack, or we faced an angry parent. We pushed, fought and toppled each other, making a muddy mess and having fun because when the windy season came along, the loose sand stung your skin and filled every crevice. Doors and windows were kept shut in the heat, but with the oddly-shaped building material, the gaps and spaces were no match for the high winds and sand. It was us against the elements during every season, as we would find out.

Shacks were erected in no time, and the new tenants moved in, meeting neighbours and settling in. Our one big boxed house was divided into four smaller squares, creating a kitchen, lounge or dining room area, and two bedrooms. There were usually no doors inside the shack, and none in ours, so we used a piece of patterned cloth in the doorways to allow some privacy. Not that it gave much privacy anyway. The yards were huge, so a family might have extra smaller shacks to house friends or relatives. There was much community love around us, it seemed.

Despite the different shapes and exteriors, the shacks were filled with almost identical ornaments and stuff for daily living. Every dining room had a sideboard or cabinet for identical or mismatched crockery and cutlery, set aside for visitors and Sunday meals. There was always that one good set of cups and saucers, side and large plates, shining crockery, a salad bowl and dessert bowls stacked away or on show. Most days we used our favourite chipped plates, mugs, cups and saucers, in different colours and sizes.

Each family member had his or her own special eating utensil, and enamel cups and plates were the norm for everyday use. Items were used until they literally fell apart or broke, as we saved on just about anything and everything. One teaspoon was passed around and used to stir all cups of tea, before I knew coffee existed. Fights broke out when a cup of tea was stirred before a cup of coffee, with a hope of returning the annoying favour later.

Any free space on the sideboards was covered in black-and-white family photos, real or otherwise, of ancient ancestors, living or dead, along with religious pictures and a Bible text to bless this humble home. Ornaments and ashtrays sat on pretty hand-sewn or crocheted doilies. Even if no one smoked, there were the token ashtrays. Walls were decorated with framed family photos, new or faded pictures depicting Jesus as a child or as an adult with his mother, Mary. No wall was without mirrors in many different shapes and sizes, while the butterfly-shaped mirrors offered you a glimpse of yourself during the day. At night or during heavy thunderstorms, our parents made us turn all the mirrors, so they faced the walls. Superstitious over something.

The lounge also had a table to fit the room, which usually sat four, the chairs in place, and only used for those noted guests. Homemade wooden stools or drums were carried along from pillar to post to provide one's own seating, depending on the occasion. One had to ask permission to sit on the "good chairs" from the dining room. Really now? Any other chairs or stools we owned came in different designs, colours, makes, models and sizes. The richer folk owned couches which matched in every aspect.

Most people used wooden stools or overturned drums for everyday use. Our good furniture was reserved only for weddings, parties, and funerals, as families borrowed and loaned furniture and other utensils to create a good impression, I would learn. People took handouts as owners of new or more posh chairs were upgraded. To me, at my young age and understanding, the social status among the poor souls around me thrived.

The kitchen was filled with makeshift cupboards, tables, and working surfaces, all made of wood or aluminium, of course. With no electricity in the shack, the commonly used cooking device was the Primus stove. A Swedish factory mechanic called Frans Wilhelm Lindqvist, who used the handheld blowtorch as a reference, developed this pressurized-burner kerosene or paraffin operated stove in 1892. It had a brass bottom and a 'burner top' supported by three legs. Those brass bottoms had to be kept shining and were dismantled and cleaned on kitchen cleaning day. The smell of paraffin clung to your hands for ages.

Naturally, we all owned one or more of these little burners to cook many pots at a time. With the uneven floors, all tables, chairs, and working surfaces were padded underfoot as a heavy or misplaced step sent everything toppling over. For that reason, sitting, walking and moving about was a gentle affair, especially at night, until all things were fixed into place. There was never a dull moment in any shack, as visitors and guests sent teacups and biscuits flying around the place.

With no electricity, most meals and food were bought, cooked and eaten on the same day, or one asked the neighbours to store their perishables in their fridge. How cool was that? Families would lend and borrow from each other all the time, be it food items, furniture, cash or a section of the daily newspaper to check up on the classifieds. We were informed if their fridge was full or playing up, so other arrangements could be made. We were all very neighbourly.

Daily meals were fine as we ate anything that was available, but the big Sunday meal was a different and bigger affair. Rice, sometimes different types of meat, vegetables, and a treat of jelly, custard, and tinned fruit would follow. Naturally, the amount and variety of food depended on the finances. The food saved for dinnertime was covered with a few tablecloths, and whoever walked by would swat at the flies buzzing around the food. The stray cats and dogs kept a hungry vigil at the doorway. All food that had to be kept cold would be sent to a neighbour until dinnertime.

The only proper table in the place had an old or used plastic or cloth cover during the week. On Sunday only, the plastic one was kept in place in case of food spills. Mind you, no one sat at the dining table to eat any meal, Sunday or not. Someone dished up for you, we grabbed a plate and on sunny days sat and ate under the shade of the trees, tossing bones and leftovers to the dogs and cats milling about.

These scavenging mongrels moved from house to house looking for scraps. We gathered anywhere in the house except to sit around or at the family table. We also had no qualms about taking our meal, climbing over the fence and sitting with our friends while eating. If you came back with the spoon and plate, they told you. No one around me used a knife and fork to eat meals. The uneven floors in all the rooms were covered in linoleum, either the same design or different pieces scavenged or bought from wherever. Nothing was wasted, as people would offer it to others before discarding or binning it.

The linoleum had to be kept shiny and polished all year round. The only carpet or mats I knew of were at the front and back door to wipe your shoes before entering. These carpeted squares were brought in at night in case they went missing. Even the poor stole from the poor. The black rubber car mats were the token image outside many a wooden front door.

Stray dogs and cats slept on the doorstep during the nights; sometimes a sleepyhead stepped on sleeping animal. These mongrels sometimes left a good-sized mound of droppings, which we unwittingly stepped into. The best mat was saved for the floor near our parents' bed, and it was shoved under the bed during the day. One was not allowed to use it at all, and this meant a cold floor for the kids first thing in the morning. Parents did not always treat us that delicately.

Kids would always be sent to collect the daily paper from this uncle or that aunt, and so news travelled from shack to shack. 'Share and share alike' was a motto for us perhaps, living as a family in our shack surrounded by our neighbours in this strange place and on a street with no name. Our life seemed good despite the odd-looking home, yet I knew no different. The spaces set aside for sleeping were crammed with one or two single beds, and the thin mattress made from foam or "coir"—a natural fibrous material from the husk of a coconut found between the hard-internal shell and outer coat of the fruit. It is used to make floor and doormats, brushes and, of course, our hardened mattresses.

We shared beds with siblings or parents and on those extra hot days, sleeping areas, beds and linen were spring-cleaned and debugged. The coir in the mattresses was good if it stayed dry and mite free but tell that to the rain and bed bugs. We also had to blame a bed wetter until they outgrew their social malady. A good night's sleep was not always a guarantee in the shack. Mattresses neatly stacked up against the wall absorbing the sunlight were a common sight in the neighbourhood. As they became lumpy and uncomfortable with overuse, the thinner ones got used as a settee in the dining room. Some were kept around in the yard to be used by man and animal alike. Using the worn-out mattresses as a play or rest area, it was strange that no fleas bothered us then. Most yards had a similar gathering spot as we sat and gossiped, played games or just watched the street. No one could keep us away from the dirty pile of mattresses. Fresh replacements were happily welcomed.

Within our little space, we huddled together, trying to keep things comfortable, if not as bearable as possible. With no jobs, my parents were always at home. From these early days, the proximity and tightly knit sleeping arrangements would have a huge impact on our social interaction, especially mine. Looking back, everyone in the shacks around us shared the same conditions, and I had no idea how they lived behind their closed doors, but I can explain how we did. For as long as I can recall, my dad had a persistent cough and it always got worse at night time. He smoked a pipe throughout the day, coughed all night and kept a small container close by into which he spat. This never stopped him despite his restlessness and not to mention our own disturbed sleeping pattern.

My mother was a social smoker at the time, which didn't help her asthma either, but she soon gave it up. When it came to bedtime, my sister and mother shared a sleeping room. My father, brother, and I shared the other room and being smaller, I got the short end of the coir mattress. I got sent to the foot end of the bed with my brother or if we had a foot fight, I was kicked out of bed, which meant I ended up sleeping at my dad's feet.

In the small room, his coughing and snoring kept us awake as we drifted in and out of sleep. When the snoring got too loud, my poor mother came along to nudge him out of the snoring fit. Funny how the coughing and wheezing disappeared when the sun made its appearance.

From that young age, I never knew my parents to sleep in the same room or in the same bed. Not that I knew parents should share a bed or a room, and I saw nothing odd or wrong about that, and assumed this happened in every shack or home.

My dad woke early to sit somewhere in the yard, prepare his tobacco pipe and drink a cup of tea. There he would stay for most of the day unless something had to be sorted out. He called out to us if he needed anything. Usually, it was for a fresh cup of tea, to pick up the newspaper, or bring his little transistor radio. Before I even knew he was a keen gardener, his position under a tree was already a staple fixture as visitors came to join him in the shade. They sat, chatted, listen to horse racing results on the radio. I noticed that sometimes they drank something other than tea or coffee. It was a special home brew or drink called Umqombothi.

Umqombothi is the Xhosa word for beer made from maize or corn, maize or sorghum malt, yeast, and water. Commonly found in South Africa, it is rich in Vitamin B. This beer has a heavy and distinct sour aroma and less than three percent alcohol, though too much of it made the elders slightly intoxicated. It also had a thick, creamy gritty consistency from the maize, leaving a bad aftertaste for those demanding a sip.

After too much Xhosa beer, Dad was unsteady on his feet and only left his low stool for toilet breaks or when nagged by my mother. He would sit under the tree, speak to himself or back chat the voices on the radio, much to my mother's annoyance as she berated his drinking that horrible beer. He was in no way schizophrenic, may I add. There he would stay well into the night, the glow of his pipe showing up as he puffed away, ignoring all pleas to come inside and sleep. This would go on for hours, and we knew his snoring would be much worse than the coughing. No matter how much my mother asked him to drink or smoke less, her words fell on deaf ears. My dad was not a violent man after too much home brewed beer, just stubborn and obstinate, and this was both funny and trying at times.

The doors of the shacks were cut in half, the top part kept open during hot days and to keep or stop stray dogs and cats walking in to steal food. Well, cats perched around as if they lived there and waited for food snippets. No bin was needed to dispose of leftover food. We scraped and emptied plates to the waiting cats and dogs outside the door. We watched them fight over the morsels and if the greedy mongrels were busy elsewhere, we left the food as they would come snooping around later. It was on a first come, first served basis. Sometimes we would search for our favourite or take the weaker dog or cat aside and feed it the leftovers. I had no idea who these animals belonged to or where they came from, but we were both cruel and kind to them.

Who needed a special pet when we had so many around the place? We needed them as much as they needed us. The closed bottom half also kept the snakes out, but they slithered between the cracks and spaces of the building materials used. Finding the odd slippery intruder in the shack was par for the course in summer. We always checked when a dog or cat sounded agitated around the place. In most cases they were having a go at a snake in the yard. We were told they were harmless but took no chances. It had to be killed and that was the exciting part as we hopped around, men and dogs in the mix. Most of the time, the snake got away and some of us were left with bruises from missed or deliberate hits from sticks and canes.

As man and animals tried to make ends meet from day to day, I became accustomed to my surroundings, how everything worked in our home and some of those around us. The children from the shacks started to explore areas outside their yard and make a path across the tarred road, which led to a completely different cultural and social setting. My father's little radio told us that Raindrops Keep Falling on my Head was the number one song in the singles chart, while the Jackson Five were just beginning to kick-start their career, and my life was about to get much more interesting. Welcome to the 1970's.

Chapter 4: a very public washing inconvenience

Since there were neither running hot water nor private bathing areas, we opted for a hidden space at the back of the shack or yard for those purposes, or rooms were vacated to allow some privacy. During winter months, my siblings squabbled over the available hot water, since heating a pot of water took some time. My mother was mindful of paraffin usage, so one pot of water had to do. The 'top and tail' ritual before school was often done in semi-dark rooms or the outside toilet if one felt brave enough. Winter weather around our shack was still warm. It was not uncommon to see someone bathing behind a shack as they tried to preserve some modesty from prying eyes.

Our bathing utensil was usually a round or square bright coloured plastic basin. There were no long soaking baths for us back then. Body and basin sizes meant you either stood and had a quick wash or sat until the water got cold. Well, most of the time only your bottom was in the basin while your feet hung over the side. Privacy and decency were not a priority if we had a good wash and scrub. On good days, a sibling or parent topped up the cooling water, or you stomped back and forth to get more hot water. Asking a neighbour to heat a pot or two was not uncommon either.

It was all about saving paraffin for the stoves. Our wash rag of choice was any piece of cloth from old clothing items, or towels cut into smaller pieces. For a good old deep clean body scrub, 'coir' from the mattresses came in handy. The plastic mesh bags that oranges were sold in also did the trick. Boy did it leave you tingling when a parent decided your neck, or the back of your knees needed a good scrub. Your friends were happy to wash your back and neck, often drawing blood or screams of pain and a subsequent naked fight in the sand. Cleanliness was next to forwardness as adults or kids assisted each other in keeping clean. Semi or full nudity was no big deal around our shacks, and no one batted an eyelash or eyelid.

Our meagre supply of clothing was washed in the same way. Hot or cold water into a basin or two, then left to soak for a while, depending on how dirty they were or on your mother's mood. Bleach or "Jik" was used for off-white clothing, since nothing stayed white for long due to the mud and red sand. Everyone reeked of bleach on washing day, as we all joined in the washing, rinsing and hanging of the clean washing. With no washing machines, our hands and feet had to do. Heavier items were stamped on by all and sundry, and kids came around begging to "stamp on washing" for some payment.

Blanket stomping was a huge community effort. Neighbours would ask our parents if they could loan the kids to help, in exchange for sweets or food. No cold hard cash or in this case brown or silver cents, since most people were cash-strapped. We rinsed items the same way, stomping them under cold running water from taps. It usually turned into a game as we splashed and kicked water everywhere. We happily played tug of war as we wrung everything dry. Dropping clean wet clothing in the red sand was no fun, and fights broke out over who was to blame. It was never a dull time around the shacks as we made a game out of any activity.

Lugging washed items of clothing over lines and fences to dry, we used all available space in and around the yard. Low-hanging tree branches supported heavy blankets as the bright sun-dried laundry in record time. Kids were on guard duty for wind, rain or sand storms. It was no fun repeating the process a second time around. Retrieving torn underwear or clothing from a neighbour's yard was somewhat humiliating, unless some mongrel got to it first, rendering it totally useless. We owned few clothing items anyway, so holding on to the them was paramount. Kind people brought back items blown into their yard by a sandstorm to the rightful owners. Even in our shack and shabby living conditions, parents made sure we looked clean and presentable as best we could with what was available to us.

We had no private wash area, but we had a private place when it came to the man-made and self-managed toilet. If you are eating and reading this, I apologize. There was a tinier shack at the back of the yard with a hole in the ground, a bucket in the hole. This served as a lavatory – you get the idea – and it had to be emptied at some point, as there was no proper sewage system around us at the time. I won't dwell too much on this. Keep it clean, I say. At night, we used a bucket to empty full bladders, and this was emptied across the road or in some corner of the yard. For fun, you opened the top part of the door and sprayed the sleeping dogs and cats with warm piss. We blamed it on being scared to go out in the dark when caught out.

Having a runny tummy was no fun either. With minimal street lighting, and parents wanting us to save candles and paraffin, you had to dash out, do your business and race back. Wary of spiders and snakes in the dark, it meant a rushed cleaning job before racing back to bed, only to be told to get back out to get rid of a smell. It was easier to clean your backside under running water than go into the dark, smelly toilet.

For the times when nature triumphed over speed, it was about a quick duck out of the door and on one's haunches to do the job, staring into the darkness ahead, your little mind playing tricks on you as the trees cast shadows all round. The stray dogs trying to sniff at you did not make things any easier. Once done, one walked bent over, ass in air to clean up before going back inside. The thought of an early morning wake-up call to retrieve and hide the evidence made for a fretful slumber. Scooping up the dried evidence in a spade, one dumped it into the bush across the road. Imagine being hit by a car while carrying a spade full of shit, dry or otherwise! A newly scraped spot in the sand was testament to your dirty deed. That piece of bush across the road was a prime dumping site for buckets full of number ones and twos, otherwise called piss and shit. Hold this thought for a later revelation.

Naturally, a toilet had to have toilet roll, as I would learn later in life, but as a child, it was something I knew nothing of. Any piece of paper, or whatever came in handy, as you dashed outside in the dark did the trick. Scraps of paper were scrunched to soften them for our tender bottoms. Old newspapers were the toilet roll of choice for us. The paper had to be soft and pliable but hard enough not to tear when used. Enough said!

Now you understand why newspaper collections and storage were such a necessity in most shacks. Not just to cover worktops, but also doubling as a toilet roll or sheet. We were not averse to nabbing scraps of paper from other toilets or dashing into yards for a quick call of nature. If all else failed, a rush into the bush across the road was an option as one watched for snakes and rats, while scouring the trees for a big enough leaf. Night time and a sudden dash in the dark with no time to grab some paper, left one hobbling around, ass in the air, grabbing at those big leaves. Such was life, as I knew it anyway and it created many wonderful images to store in my brain.

Chapter 5: shackled to the elements, social and climatic

For cooking, we used a Primus stove, while others had a coal stove. The former could not be left unattended as it sparked flames when pots boiled over. Fires were a risk since most building material used for the shacks was flammable. As they were built close to each other, any fire would be a disaster in the making. Sparks from the stoves, flickering or burning lamps were the other dangers. Polished linoleum over uneven floors, wobbly furniture, general clumsiness, or surprising a scavenging stray cat or dog, often sent candles or a lamp crashing to the floor. Wax and paraffin sprayed everywhere as we all jumped into action to prevent a fire, small or big. Most working surfaces had a plastic or paper cover to keep things clean. Water taps randomly placed in most of the yards allowed anyone with a hosepipe to be a fireman until the real ones came along, with a little help from everyone wielding a bucket and no water restrictions.

As I became aware of my new home and surroundings, life seemed to roll on around us. That we had no electricity, no running hot water, no proper toilet or shower areas was the least of our worries. Because of the excessive heat and humidity in Durban, coupled with the dodgy building materials used, fires were our biggest worry.

The lamps and candles we used to light our way in the dark caused friction among those managing the meagre finances.

Paraffin was not cheap, we were told, and breaking any lamp was a major crime. We might borrow or lend the small stove, but the lamps were a different issue. The glass covers were a family's pride and joy, if not a status symbol in some houses. Polished and cleaned daily, they took centre stage on cabinets during the day and lighting them demanded the utmost concentration. Preserving the glass cover was all important, so these lamps got used sparingly since the paraffin and wick were a bit costly for a poor family.

The cheap candle, mostly white, was stuck onto broken saucers, plates, upended cups or glassed or forced into empty bottle openings, creating a stream of dried wax down the sides. New candles were placed over hardened wax, creating fancy designs. Similar waxy figures and silhouettes became an art craze in the 90's, but we had it going in the seventies.

Paraffin rations and candle overuse were frowned upon and we had no say over when it was time for lights out. My mother put out candles and lamps and we chatted in the darkness, telling lame jokes, rehashing games and the usual scary antics until we fell asleep. Sharing a bed with an older brother was not easy as we fought and bickered over everything. Space, cold feet, hogging the covers, kicking or pinching each other with our toes were the main ones.

Just a quick jump to my immediate surroundings. The many cold-water taps were not always reliant as we learned about storing water for a rainy day. Every house owned a huge barrel or clean drum to store water just in case the taps ran dry, or to help if a neighbour's water supplies ran out. Buckets, pots, and drums got filled with water and passed over fences.

As the seasons changed, fruit trees around the place beckoned us with their tasty loot and we enjoyed everything from a mango, guava, pawpaw or papaya, passion fruit or granadilla as we knew it, avocado, lemon, banana, peach, mulberry, raspberry, grapes and the sour fruit of the loquat tree, all the way from China. What we did not have in our yard, we happily snatched from overhanging trees or entered yards with intent to grab and run. Those strong gale force winds came in handy sometimes if kicking tree stumps did not work. A fruit paradise indeed and my father added the vegetable spice to it.

The hardy soil across the road was suitable for a vegetable patch and a crop favourite, maize. My father had a patch cleaned and planted any seeds, shoots or pips he bought or was given. Beetroot, onions, potatoes, tomatoes, carrots, pumpkins, spinach, beans and radish to name a few. He sold and bartered and when times were hard, there was always vegetable stew or soup to be made. He spent all day and early evening sitting in his garden, content, happy and isolated, bouts of coughing alerting people passing along the pathway. Sometimes animals or humans raided the patch at night, leaving a forlorn figure to clean up the damage and sigh at the injustice of it all. All they had to do was ask, since he was not a stingy person at all. The harsh weather conditions were a different issue. Most crops seemed to thrive very well there, as I remind you of those many spades and buckets we emptied in the now cleared patch of garden. Everything tasted so good too!

Other than his vegetables, my father, being a farm-raised kid, was not scared of hard work despite his back problem. A few cages were erected at the back of our shack to house chickens, rabbits and guinea pigs. Two of the three were destined for a pot and the other a furry pet. Poor as we were, it never registered that people would buy some guinea pig for a pet. The chicken eggs were a bonus as man heckled angry hen during egg collection. My father was industrious in his own right, as we helped him around the garden and cages. These too were not totally safe from thieving man and animal. Cats and snakes were the main culprits.

It was the first time I recall seeing white mice and not understanding why people treated them differently to the many grey ones around the place. They were kept in cages and were people-friendly, compared to the big grey rats that scurried around the shacks. It was strange indeed but we there were so many rodent nests around the place, we stole a newborn mouse and kept it as a plaything until our parents caught us out. It was fun having them swim in a bowl of swirling water to see which one won the battle. Not a cruel bone in our little bodies.

Together with the guinea pigs, mice, rabbits, stray cats and dogs around, who needed a pet animal? One dog took my fancy and I named her Tessa. I had no idea where she came from or if she had an owner, but her hazel eyes and brown coat were gorgeous. She was very tame, unlike most stray dogs that passed through yards. The term pet was not one I would know and understand for many years.

With poverty all around us, we appeared to be happy and content in our own space or shared spaces in some cases. Petty sales from our stock of chickens, rabbits, eggs and vegetables kept our bellies full. Our shack was clean, homely and we had a roof of sorts over our heads, water and decent enough clothing. The external elements we faced made life a bit interesting and sometimes unbearable.

Constant heavy rain, gale force winds and excessive heat or humidity were our main challenges.

Durban is extremely humid and hot in summer, and it was torture from the moment the bright sun showed its face. Our shack built from asbestos and aluminium turned into a sauna, staying humid throughout the day and well into the night—if not all through the night and into next morning. The odd breeze made an appearance, we had no fans, and thus suffered. Windows were kept shut against relentless flies and a million mosquitoes. The lack of a proper sewerage system was the main attraction for these critters no doubt.

Sales of insect-catching strips peaked, and they dotted walls and roofs of every shack, but despite the deadly insect sprays used, nothing saved us from their buzz, bite or sting. The nights seemed to drag and with it, our torture. We could not wait for sunrise. As adults reclined in the shade, we hosed each other down or sat in huge plastic tubs filled with cold water. Our own private tiny splash pool. Fights broke out as we kid jostled for our turn, tired grumpy sleepy parents angrily disconnecting hose pipes to restore peace and quiet. And so, the wheel of humidity turned slowly as we prayed for summer to come to an end.

Our prayers were answered, well not really since we had nothing to do with it, but the place cooled down and sleeping became much easier. The flies and mosquitoes never left, they were always around anyway, but we only noticed them during high summer. No matter what the season, Durban is known for its frightening thunderstorms. Loud, harsh thunder and fierce lightning was as bad as the summer heat as our parents warned us about being struck by lightning. With our flimsy homes and combustible materials at risk of fire from all angles once again and with tall trees around us, we were sitting ducks, I guess. During the day, we tempted fate, darting from one tree to the next, muddied and dirty as rain, thunder and lightning flashed down from the sky. Parents promised us a thrashing as we played outside at being daredevils.

Come rain, wind, sun or thunderstorm, we suffered in our shack. During heavy rains, water dripped through gaps or openings between the mix-matched materials that kept the flimsy shack together. Holes in the roof were common, and we used any container to catch the steady drip of water. Steel or plastic pots and buckets dotted floors, beds, and furniture. The noise of dripping water kept us awake as much as we had to empty the semi full containers. Cue another bout of minimal sleep.

Furniture was rearranged, old clothing strewn across the floor to absorb the rest or to prevent us slipping. Let me not even start about the gale force winds, hailstorms and ice battering the roof and windows. They were as scary and terrifying as the thunderstorms. Temporary plastic covers rattled as swirling winds flapped curtains around our heads in the dark. The rain, the noise, the panic, the fear of fire and any damage to her home kept my mother, and many others, awake most of the night. Our parents did everything to keep us from floating away, and after the rain, we counted our blessings until the next downpour. Is it possible that these early childhood weather-induced irregular sleeping patterns have played some part in my disturbed sleeping disposition as an adult?

We lived amongst fruit trees in a neighbourhood full of mixed, colourful shacks and characters as we weathered storms that came our way. Adults and kids in harmony as they lived from day to day. Since my parents were home all day, my two siblings had already begun primary school, although I have almost no memory of them leaving me alone for most of the day. It is indeed strange that some things are clearer than others, and I cannot recall any friends I had at this time, nor that I even had cousins living close by.

That some people lived in real brick houses next to our shack, was another vague fact locked in my memory somewhere. An actual house I cannot recall but I do recall that bricks and stones were part of our playgrounds. Perhaps, I had forgotten or 'blanked out' some details about myself or my life from around this time. Why on earth would I want to do that? I never forgot my first real beating and the memory of bricks.

Despite having fruit trees in our yard, the fruit on another tree always looked tastier and juicier, even if it was in another yard. We wanted ripe lemons from a neighbour's tree, but it meant we had to straddle an unfinished brick wall in the process.

Sliced lemons covered in salt and curry powder were a treat we enjoyed. I had to sit on the wall, while someone held my foot as I leaned towards the tree to make a grab for the fruit. It was an easy job, but the noise must have alerted the resident dog and it came charging towards the wall. The barking startled us all, my foot was released, and I tumbled head first over the wall and onto a pile of bricks. Everyone scattered on the other side as the homeowner found a bleeding, crying child with a barking dog at his feet. There was blood everywhere from a cut just over my left eye and right wrist.

I vaguely heard shouting for help and ambulance above my own howling, but once I was handed to my angry parents, I knew what awaited me. Angry at the theft and injury, I felt the sting over my pants bottom as the ambulance raced to our shack, and a vague memory of a trip to the place of my birth, Addington Hospital. Someone did a hatchet job on my wounds and I carry the scars to this day. I must have played the docile patient role down to the letter T. Crime came at a price they said, but the little coloured boy never took the advice to heart.

We found ways to keep us busy and entertained, playing hide and seek, a bit less wary of where we hid, hopscotch in the sandy soil, drawing lines on roads, while dodging traffic and arguing over positions, points and partners. Ropes used for skipping, high and long jump were stolen or bartered, as cheating created scrabbles and fights. Generally, most kids were active throughout the day. The weather dictated our play and home times, angry parents waving belts in our direction. We straggled or bolted home, making up excuses as we entered the doorway. Sometimes, one ran to the toilet, claiming an upset tummy, refusing offers of cod liver, castor oil or Brooklax. We rejoiced at our friends screams, as they were set to task for being disobedient.

After exhausting play areas, our beady eyes focused on the bush across the road as people used the trodden path and disappeared beyond the shrubbery. We found shops, stalls and markets, owned by Indians. Surprised and excited, we found Raj Mahal or Natraj, was an ideal Indian market place for buying day-to-day necessities. There was a tiny cinema house, which recycled western and karate movies, until the new ones came along.

Chapter 6: curries and bunnies: an indian affair with natraj

After discovering all paths through the brush led to the Indian markets, it became part of a daily detour. Natraj was a vibrant busy market with small shops, cafes and stalls selling fruit, food, meat, vegetables, clothing and household goods one might need on a day to day basis. Scruffy barefoot kids and scavenging animals loitered around for a mislaid, dropped or unattended delicacy. Kids worked in groups to distract owners as others fled with whatever they could grab. Usually it was something sweet or edible. Stall owners kept a beady eye on most kids since it was obvious we had no money to spend, our parents seldom entrusting us to go out and buy anything. Older boys took the money, offering to run the errand, but they pocketed the cash and stole the items. Not every barefoot ruffian was a thief, mind you. Though seen as a game, it was really classified as theft.

Keeping a low profile for a few weeks or hiding behind our mother's skirts, there was no way we could resist the fresh smelling spices, cooked food and savouries. One had never tasted such spicy delicious food before and despite being warned of eating too much curry, we ate as much as we could lay our hands on. Anything to stop the noise in our hungry bellies. Food was food.

At this market, I had my first taste of the baked or fried Indian savoury known as the samosa or somosa. It was the best thing since sliced bread, but then they added even tastier meals and foods for us to buy. After mild stews and barely hot curries, this was heaven to our palates. Before long, we made friends with the Indian kids whose aunt, uncle or parents owned the stalls, meaning free food at the end of closing. Judging the visits right, we were more than happy to relieve them of any leftover foods and sweets. Nothing could go to waste and they were very happy to share as we carted stuff home to share our good fortune. Then I fell in love with my all-time favourite meal.

Breyani or biryani is an Urdu word derived from the Persian language, and there is a theory that "birinj" means rice while "biryan" is to fry or roast. Whatever the origin, this mixed rice dish was simply delicious. It was hard not to lick the plates as we did at home. It was strange to watch them eat food with their hands and fingers, as we used spoons. At home we annoyed our parents with our useless attempts at eating with our fingers, the food going everywhere except into our mouths. I still saw no one use a knife or fork. Although the adult Indians sat around a table and ate, the kids sat outside to enjoy the meal.

After the spicy samosas and biriyani meals, it was the turn of the bunny chow or just bunny: a hollowed-out loaf of bread filled with curry and eaten with clean hands and fingers, naturally. A true South African and Durban original is our bunny. Opinions on how they came about ranged from sugar cane workers having their vegetable curries added to hollowed out bread to that it was easier to sell as a takeaway meal for those races not allowed to enter certain shops. During the apartheid years, non-whites were not allowed to carry cutlery. The traditional Indian meal was roti and beans, and since the former broke easily, the hollowed-out bread was a good idea. Whoever started the bunny needs a medal indeed.

The small Indian community with its many strange intoxicating smells, bright materials, great tasting food and friendly people, despite us trying to rob them at every corner, was a welcome distraction from our tiny shacks. Our parents knew where to find us, but we had nothing to fear as everyone seemed to live in near perfect harmony. Other than the odd beating for being naughty and disrespectful, my fall onto the bricks and I was now a scarred thief, we appeared happy with our lot in life. It seemed a better life than the farm my dad grew up on.

From my first shack and our Natraj exploits, memories are more visual rather than an emotional connection. The shack I called home is a clear vision in my mind, yet I sat and ate in houses made of stone and cement and have very little memory of what they looked like on the inside. Not knowing where we came from before moving into the shack does bother me. I hope I get the information to share with you before I get to complete the book. Happy, free-spirited and content, we had no idea our little haven was under threat at all.

Chapter 7: duranta road or rainbow chickens: a hotbed of shifting sands

Suddenly, our parents were thrown into a state of chaos over rumours about 'proper' houses being built and get ready to be evacuated as they intended to build new roads, flats or houses. Our shacks would be demolished after all the hard work, but the new place would have electricity, hot and cold tap water, an inside toilet and bathroom. It sounded like heaven to our parents' ears but the fear of the unknown always sent my poor mother into a state. We had no idea where the new houses were or if they would separate us from friends and neighbours in the process. Given no option, packing had to be done after being told to take only what we really needed. Which was odd as we had so little idea what kind or size of building we were going to live in.

We sorted and packed our belongings in between breaks to gossip and muse over this new turn of events. Why were they moving us suddenly? I had not yet started a school year, so the shack had been my home for less than two years. We would miss the Indian shops and markets, their food and possibly be moved away from friends or never see them again. The strong brick walls and windows would protect us from all kinds of weather, they kept telling us, and the packing continued as we waited for the day of reckoning. We also had no idea who was going to move us out of the place.

Sadly, since it was sudden and with little warning, there was a mass slaughter and feeding frenzy of chickens and rabbits alike. Selling and donating the guinea pigs, we joined everyone else as we discarded, bartered and traded in preparation for the new home. We scavenged among discarded items as we waited for it all to go down.

One day, without much warning, huge bulldozers, vans and trucks moved in. Taking over the single tarred road, vehicles and men seemed to be everywhere before getting down to business. Everyone scurried around trying to remove and safeguard their tiny kids and meagre bounty. Assuming they would evacuate us all before demolishing the shacks, these guys were not here to hang around. Standing aside, scared and nervous, with everything we owned or could afford to carry, the huge noisy bulldozers rammed into the shacks, razing them to the ground in front of our eyes. I remember those huge steel wheels on the machines, or gun-da-gun-da's – as we called them, yet strangely I cannot recall the men who drove them, but they lifted us onto the giant cars as they wrecked our homes. Being surrounded by mostly Indian or Coloured males in my tiny life so far, one would think seeing a White or Black male breaking down my house might have stuck in my head somewhere. Everything was a dusty haze as the noise and fear of the unknown cloaked our parents, while we saw it as an adventure.

They made it seem like a fun game by involving the kids while they tore down their parents, handiwork in the meantime. It was still the only home we knew. Even if it was made of dangerous and useless materials, it was still our home. We all were left facing the huge pile of rubble after the dust and noise had settled. We were homeless, if only for those few minutes or hours it took to cart us away from a place we had got to call home. Waving goodbye to the first few who piled onto the trucks and vans, we said our farewell to those who were not going anywhere, no doubt with a promise or hope that we meet again. For now, it was time to say goodbye to the street with no name.

After the shock of seeing our homes broken down, the kids were offered to ride along to cart people to the new homes and return for the next bunch. So, it turned out that we were all going to the same place, which was good news. Parents allowed us to go along, and we came back all excited about the new brick houses, no doubt. Having never been in a car up until this point, I had no concept of how far we drove before we offloaded and went back. Once the last stragglers were collected and deposited into their new abode, we all breathed a sigh of relief and took stock of our brand-new surroundings. Sadness was mixed with a bit of eagerness to start the new chapter in our lives.

Well, the new house was virtually a stone's throw away from our demolished shacks, it appeared. We did live in a road with a name after all. Duranta Road had already been surrounded by many other proper homes, which meant people had been staying there for some time. It was not so new after all, except for many rows of flat-roofed houses meant for us. All front doors, there was no back door, all faced each other, and bar the two-toned pastel-painted walls, everything looked identical. Once the excitement and stress of the move subsided, we finally had a roof over our heads and people came to meet and welcome us to the Barracks or Rainbow Chickens, as we all got to know it. How, who and when they baptized these new digs is a mystery, as they resembled an army base, apparently, not that I had seen one before.

While we were happy, our parents seemed less enthused about the barracks. Everything smelt fresh, clean and new as we ran from room to room exploring, not as if we had far to run. A dining room or lounge area, two tiny bedrooms, a tiny kitchen, which was next to a tinier toilet and snow-white bath. Not fussed about the layout, we were so happy with everything. The toilet with a flushing handle, which was a first to those from shack homes, bath, hot and cold-water taps, and light switches were a pure delight.

Dirty fingers clicked and flushed, marvelling at the bright lights and gushing water until annoyed parents demanded we stop wasting lights and water. Walls were so thin, we heard our neighbours' kids being reprimanded as well. Were we going to pay for using running water and bright lights? This was news to us but for now it was only fair to play around until we got used to it.

From the outside in, we had more windows than the shack, but every house shared one long aluminium sheet for a roof. There was a small sand patch at the front door to demarcate your private space. There would be no garden for my father, alas. The same soft sand and grass patches surrounded most of the places. There were some cemented steps leading to homes on a lower level, but most of the time we scurried down grass slopes and banks. It appeared they built the homes on soft shifting sands, almost like the beach. Except we had no sea in front of us.

It did not take long to unpack and settle in, since we had so little. What we needed for the house, we might get as handouts from relatives, friends or strangers. The cement on the floor was cool under our feet and our cheap wooden furniture looked ill-placed in its new setting. Refurnishing would take some time but there was no hurry since we were going nowhere in a hurry. Those monthly grants would have to be treated with care now that we had a proper house to uphold and pay for it seemed. Nothing was a free handout, even to the poor and unemployed.

Mass unpacking had to be done, curtains or sheets covered windows, and our rickety wooden furniture looked out of place on the new shiny cemented floor. Refurnishing would have to wait for handouts from relatives, friends, or strangers who were lucky or privileged enough to upgrade and furnish throughout the year.

Glad we still had the same neighbours and friends a new house, and by the time we took stock of everything around us, it was far too late. After the first few seasons had made their presence felt, there was a strong sense of déjà vu. Well, I shall not rehash the scenarios, but basically, we had been moved from the fat into the fire.

Cutting this long story short, the aluminium roof increased the volume of heavy rains and hailstones. The brick walls provided less better protection from the loud thunder, lightning flashes, only enhancing the sound and echo. We might as well have been in the shack. The rain turned the sand to pure mud and we struggled to get in and out of the house. With no protection from the watery sludge and rain, we put padding under the door to keep water and mud out. Rain water seeped into the walls, keeping them damp for weeks to follow. My mum and dad really suffered, and he smoked all day, to cough and snore all night.

There were leaks from the roof and we resorted to pots, bowls, basins, moving things around and prayed everything stayed in place after any storm. The steel on the roof created the sauna effect once again and we fought flies and mosquitoes in the night. During the day, we hopped, skipped and jumped over hot scorching sand with a pair of flip-flops or sandals on our dusty feet. This was the first time we wore any kind of footwear during the day. Our cheap plastic footwear broke easily, got sewn or strung back into one piece, and worn until a new pair came along. To this day, I hate and will not wear a sandal or flip-flop.

Our parents complained we were no better off here than the shacks when things got a bit too much, but we had a real house at least. It could not burn down easily and there was no need to go outside in bad weather to use the toilet, which was a plus. So, it was bad at times, but the better option in the end. Whoever built the barracks had not been thinking about our comfort or the well-being of those who were not healthy.

Not everyone in the new place had come from the same area, and we got to meet them along the way. Directly opposite us lived a family with a different skin, hair, and eye colour which seemed at odds with everyone else. Pale and fair, they spoke Afrikaans, like my mother. Looking back, I would classify them as whites, but I had no idea that we were any different in any way. There were just a very white-skinned family, and all sounded like my mother.

Yet, further along the same row lived a family whose gorgeous black, dark skin was a strong contrast to our direct neighbours' pale complexions, and who spoke English. With a good dose of Portuguese genes in their blood, how did they end up living among us in the barracks? Not that I expected them to live anywhere else, yet it seemed everyone knew each other from somewhere, except the family who spoke Afrikaans, who did at times look completely out of place.

Weather dramatics and their aftermaths only made us stronger and resilient to fight or help each other around the place. Our rainbow chicken homes were nothing like coops at all, but it sure felt like one at times. Living on top of each other, or literally side by side, we pretty much knew everyone's business. The paper-thin walls were not meant to contain angry loud voices.

The term barracks suited my new home, since they looked like a soldiers' dormitory. Did you know the word barracks has French origins from the Catalan word "barraca" which refers to a temporary shelter or hut? Did that mean we were not here for a long time? Or was that pure wishful thinking? Now we had a place with an address and the demolished shack would fade yet remain a vivid memory all my life. I was a small child who had no idea that my parents and those around us had no say in where they wanted to live. Someone put us there without consulting them, and for now it had to do. Duranta Road had finally become a reality.

Chapter 8: tara road, fatcakes and weather mishaps

With all the excitement of relocating, we missed the monstrosity not very far away. A sprawling oil refinery, right in our back or front yard. Great big rows of steely silver pipes stretched for miles, spouting black smoke high into the air, day and night. Wire fencing kept the public away as heat, smoke, the never-ending humidity and smells wafted over the barracks. We breathed in petrol, oil, and gas fumes, those with breathing and chest problems suffering the most. Despite providing employment for many people in the area, breathing in those fumes daily could not have been a good thing if you were on the other side of the fence. The refinery processed tons of crude oil and millions of litres of petrol.

Heavy thick smoke always hung in the air, loud popping sounds precipitated huge red flames gushing high into the air. As spectacular as it looked, we were warned of fires and explosions, which in turn ensured altered sleeping patterns all over again. Our ire over the seasonal hazards was combined with this daily menace. Life was not fair as every loud pop and spurt of black smoke prevented a good night's sleep and disrupted a game as we watched and waited for it to remain contained within the steel pipes.

On the other side of the huge refinery was a small hill dotted with houses and a bright blue sea hidden from our view. Tara Road separated us from the pipes, and a canal for the waste and sewage prevented us from getting any closer. At the bottom of the canal was a tiny stream in which we found tadpoles, which gave us an excuse to play in the area. No one warned us about the sewage and we screamed into the canal, laughing at the echoing it produced. Drawing childlike faces on the concrete walls before we left and searched for greener pastures to explore.

Back at the house, the thin walls cracked as we hammered nails into them to hang our pictures and clothing. Remember we had no wardrobe at the time, and everything clung to nails on the wall and behind doors. One hanger was used for multiple items, the rest being folded neatly and placed on beds and man-made wooden shelves or desks. Our house looked like its old self in no time. I still shared a bed with my brother or got kicked out to sleep at my dad's feet, while my mother and sister shared a separate room. Due to the foul air, we kept all windows closed and with my dad's snoring and coughing, it was pure torture when you added the heat and smells.

We had a proper toilet and bathroom, yet we still used crumbled newspaper to flush down the waste. After the last piece of newspaper or page from a magazine had been used, the next person had to see for themselves in an emergency, but we knew what it meant if anyone was heard shouting for help from the small ablution room. It was fun prolonging their torture and no doubt we got the same treatment sometime later.

Our Primus stoves were still used, despite having electrical sockets at our disposal. It was some time before a second-hand electrical two-plate stove entered our kitchen via a kind neighbour. This in turn was only used in emergencies and on Sundays, to save electricity. Paraffin cooking gadgets, lamps and candles still ruled, and we still used the enamel cups, plates, and mixed matched utensils as before. Everyone around me ate meals with a spoon and we never sat at the cheap dining table.

It was a brand-new house with different surroundings but the same old stale routine. It was what we all thought, yet life in the barracks would get much more interesting. With little open space or good soil for gardening, my poor father was at a loss. With a lack of good soil for gardening, they had to mix soil to allow some flowers to grow around the place. People built a fence around the area in front of their door to avoid a stampede through their plants. Suddenly it was 'my' space and 'your' yard. Now that we had a 'respectable' enough house to host visitors, relatives popped in for a visit for a day or longer. They arrived with their own blankets and mattress, and we kids were kicked off the bed to allow for guests to enjoy a single bed. We were more than happy to have a new person around, breaking the monotony of the days and nights.

My favourite drop-in relative was my Aunt Katie, a real chatterbox and a very good cook. She made nice curries, her Saturday specialty dish being the vetkoek, literally translated as fatcake. A traditional South African fried dough bread with Dutch origins, called oliebollen and usually filled with mince curry, but anything else was fine if it was hot and spicy.

That was how we liked it and the hotter the curry, the better. Aunt Katie was the first person I knew who got a monthly box of groceries, from the government they said. It did not last very long as she happily cooked her way through the contents. Atoor Kok, my grandfather from my mum's side, also made a few visits to our home. We had no idea where he came from and went back to, just like his daughter Aunt Katie, whose brother and my Uncle Robert, from Cape Town, was also someone I recall coming to our new house.

I wasn't sure what a blood uncle, aunt or relative meant since we called everyone by that prefix; I would learn the difference as I aged. People were related by sharing a common bloodline while others were given respect and honour for being an older person. There was no mixing of the blood or genetic pool at all, and if someone were just a stranger we had to be polite to them, and vice versa. News that I had many uncles, aunts, nephews and nieces living close by was a shock. With little memory of meeting anyone my age before or after moving to the barracks, I was surprised to learn that my cousins had lived with us. Our house should have been crowded, and yet I have no recollection of their presence.

My most vivid memory of a full house and human traffic was before, during and after a funeral. Not sure if I had started primary school when someone passed away. There are vague memories of a short, dark-skinned woman and they said it was Mariah, my father's mother and my grandmother. Had she lived with us before her death or, like a few other relatives, had visited and left without leaving much of an impression, I don't recall. Very odd indeed, but for days, people sat around praying, singing, and drinking cups of tea, coffee or juice, day and night. The adults seemed sad and sombre while kids hogged the biscuits, cakes, and sweets dotted around the place.

After the funeral, everyone returned to their homes and normality resumed in ours. A few family members remained on the periphery of my consciousness, but no one left any deep or lasting impressions, other than the few I had mentioned. Perhaps the fact I had not started school was a reason for the lack of memory, but I don't know why I have many clear memories of my life before moving out of the wooden shack. Luckily, friends in and around the barracks would make double sure I had ingrained memories to last for a lifetime.

Chapter 9: factions, fights and family feuds

Soon after moving into our first proper house, my school career was about to begin at the age of six. This was around 1973 and the same year Steve Biko, an anti-apartheid activist, was banned by the South African government. He was not allowed to speak to more than one person at a time, in public or to the media. Nobody could talk about or quote him in public. A mere four years later, he would die, aged 30, and there was no way of knowing how his short lifetime on earth impacted on my future. I had another year to wait before my first year of school, so in the meantime, let me explain how things unfolded around our identical block of flat roofed dwellings.

Protected in the barracks and living for the moment, we gave no thought to past or present external issues. It did not take long to settle and create a similar set up as in the shacks. New coats of paint were applied to walls, window panes and doors, making it easier to differentiate the identical row of homes. Full length doors were replaced with a top and a bottom half, to continue the past tradition of conversing with passing friends and never step outside the front door. Old habits die hard.

After living along one road, we had to navigate many streets, footpaths and short cuts to reach our destination and return home. There were larger homes, churches, snaking streets leading to schools and small convenience shops. We went around seeking new adventures with very little adult supervision, returning home tired, hungry and dirtier. Our parents had no idea we took bets on who would run past the refinery and over the hill, to collect a hand of sea sand to prove you were a daredevil. I guess the love for running had begun at this point and luckily nothing bad happened to anyone.

As new kids on the block and from the poor side of town, mixing and making friends took some time. First, they said we came from the tin shanties, our first shack homes, and now we were labelled as the kids from the barracks; either way it seemed they looked down on us. It was not a good start as fights and arguments broke out during games. It was us against them, and a favourite way to settle any misunderstanding was to throw stones at each other. As many and as big as possible, not fussed who got struck in the battle. Hitting a window or two usually sent us fleeing in all directions to avoid getting blamed. We were happy and proud to proclaim when a target got hit, but no one wanted to be the window breaker. Boys collecting stones only meant one thing.

Despite the tiny mishaps among us, we joined each other and hopped, skipped, raced, and jumped our way around the streets and yards. Tug of war, skipping, long and high jump duels coincided with all types of ball games, as we did not want to miss out. We joined one team and game after another, made up our own game if excluded and we never tired of throwing, collecting, sharing or stealing marbles, throwing tops yoyo's. I became very good at hopping, jumping, running and skipping higher, further, faster and longer than most kids could. I say that with utter conviction.

No one took much notice of me as I melted into the crowd of unkempt, barefoot, but a happy kid. Sore and sour losers broke, stole or smashed toys and things, so we improvised along the way. We jaywalked and sped away when angry drivers tried to get at us. The maze of flat homes was too daunting, and we could count on our own to watch out for us. We were too busy having the time of our life until we noticed the older kids and adults having their own kind of fun around the place, amid a different set of rules.

Everything built gradually with everyone in on the idea of cutting through the dreary days and nights on the place. I knew about the home-made beer my dad drank, and it became something of a regular habit among the old men who sat in a circle, talking, smoking their pipes and sipping from one or more jugs. It was usual to have one jug passed around in the circle, ensuring everyone had a sip. Like most drinking buddies, a mini fight had to break out over something or the other. So, for the first time, we had to watch adults bicker and argue, giggling as they stumbled around trying to maintain some dignity in the soft sand. Raised angry voices were becoming a regular habit and this was both scary and theatrical at the same time.

The presence of home brewed beer, with voices increasing in sound and excitability, began to feature most weekends. Once the beer flowed, no one cared about battery power, so the tiny transistor radios blared for most of the day and night, until someone called it a night. Soon, the music, drinking, laughing and chatting went well into the night and morning. Our neighbours' house was the designated house of excess and decadence. It was a much younger group who set out to give us all a run for our money and more in the distant future.

It started slowly but escalated rapidly before anyone could put a lid on things. There were the empty bottles on the ground, the strange smells in the air and young people making the house next door their first or second home. A constant parade of old and new faces in and out of the place. We got to know them as polite and friendly, yet we gave them a wide berth once things kicked into high gear. Parents grabbed kids and kept them indoors, locks and latches applied. We had no idea why they did that, since we wanted to hang around the party animals. They used us as barmen or waiters to replenish and retrieve their stock, while we expected something in return.

Behold if your parents saw you catering to the drinking party, there was a belt strap waiting behind a closed door, but we still took chances. The residents got used to the drinking, dancing, smoking, and laughter, often taking a bit of advantage of the situation. Debts were settled amid drunken promises while we carried, poured, refilled or collected empty cans, bottles and glasses. When no money hit our palm, a secretive stolen sip of alcohol hit the spot. Rolling about in the sand to imitate the drunken adults, annoyed our parents even more and the parties started on a Friday afternoon, ending on a Monday morning. Dwellers moaned about the noise, yet no one confronted the debauched set of party animals.

As Friday afternoon approached, the uneasy feeling of expectation hovered in the air, and increased as the party picked up swing. The strange smell filtered through open windows and so we found out about weed, marijuana, or dagga. They smoked more than they drank it seemed, which led to loud bickering followed by drunken fights or arguments. Most doors were closed and stayed shut all evening, which made them see it as a slight on their presence. They were only having fun so why did everyone avoid them, so they knocked on doors, inviting people but had to settle for a polite refusal.

We had no idea that dagga was illegal or about the effects on its users and combining it with alcohol was not a good idea. Human traffic in and out of the barracks grew to a constant and so did petty squabbles over unpaid debts, stolen drinks, cigarettes and dagga. My green-eyed friend, Carlton lived next door with his parents, his uncle was the main party animal in the place.

Our weekends became a revolving door of sheer panic, fear, anxiety and despair due to the drunk, drugged and persistent knocking on doors and windows, demanding the slightest attention. Due to the thin walls, we heard everything and stifled out giggles under the covers. Profanities and cursing ruled the night as shocked parents asked for manners and respect from everyone. Peace talks were short-lived, as camaraderie put a spanner in any serious lectures.

These late-night parties and illegal drug users changed the atmosphere in the barracks forever. Tensions were running high and when someone called the cops during a very bad fight, suddenly the whole mood changed for the worse. Things had gotten out of hand and the residents could take no more. I had never seen anyone disappear so fast in my life as semi-drunk and drugged men and boys scattered in all directions to flee from the police. Cursing and swearing at the top of their lungs, threatening to make 'mincemeat' of the culprit who rattled on them. They kicked at closed locked doors, scaling fences and jumping through open windows in the haste to avoid being seen or caught.

Relatives and loved ones pleaded with the cops to release those apprehended, promising no repeat performances, but we all knew it was a blatant lie. Those taken away would only be out a few days later to continue where they left off. So, we got to harbour and hide drug abusers from the cops almost every weekend. They braved, dared and spat at the cops in defiance, and it was quite a weekend spectacle to behold. Cops became a semi-permanent fixture to maintain peace and quiet along Duranta and Tara roads.

Garrulous neighbours rehashed the fights and dramatics with shock and disgust. The days of broken bottle heads being used to slash, cut or maim were born, but they flung anything at the opponent, breaking skin, bone and windows in the process. Incensed home owners grappled with thugs over smashed windows and it seemed we were all getting in on the action. Since we lived on top of each other, there was no escape, and we wondered when it would all come to an end. We feared the unpredictable outrage and wrath from the drug-fueled party animals and prayed they would take their parties to another place.

The young men and some women around us appeared to speak a different language to everyone else, bar the swear words. It sounded like a secret language only they could understand. We had no idea that this new type of speech or 'slang' was often used by a group of youngsters who were part of a gang. They were to be feared and to be left alone or avoided at all costs. They created a street slang as they skulked and squirmed around on their turf, calling it Wenties, the place to be.

In a very short space of time, our new houses had turned into a virtual prison. Tension and dissatisfaction hovered around every brick and sandy corner. Everyone kept their head down and dealt with the problem in the only manner they knew, silence. When and how had it all come to this? Wentworth, or Wenties, a township in the South Durban

Basin, had been an army base for British soldiers. In 1950, the Group Areas Act divided blacks, whites, Indians, and mixed ethnic people, or coloureds, which would be us, to live in separate areas in the country. Around 1960, and just before my birth, coloureds got moved to the swampy, unused land in Wentworth, the red brick homes of the white army families taken over by the new mixed-race owners. The richer ones could buy homes and property on Treasure Beach, separated from Tara Road and Wentworth by Happy Valley.

Informal settlements and tin shanties were built and demolished in 1952 and 1963, to erect the huge oil refinery in the area. Where did those people come from and where were they moved to? Since this was close to my birth in 1967, it is possible we moved from one shanty hut into that unknown road and another shack until I became aware of my surroundings. Which means my parents might have been living in Durban for quite some time, but it left me with unanswered questions.

Those living on and over the hill were safe from the drug- and alcohol-induced fights we endured. Our small Indian market area was situated in Merebank, site for the first ever Mondi Paper Mill built in 1967. Together with the oil refinery, they ensured that a constant cloud of smog, smoke, and noxious smells filled the air around us, assisted by the sea breeze, no doubt.

The soot on our skins or the gases we inhaled paled in comparison to our daily drama as things went up a notch. Openly using, pushing and selling their wares now, nothing became a secret as the users and sellers walked around with attitude, confident no one could touch them, not even the cops. Walking around with dogs straining on leashes, it was routine to stop and talk to groups of young men in the area. Gangsters and police did not see eye to eye and basically everyone felt the latter were out to get every one of us and were not to be trusted. Gangsters refused to toe the line, despite the eternal presence of the police, while the ordinary good citizen was caught in the crossfire. It was the birth of the Durban gangster in our once brand-new haven.

Weekends in the barracks usually started peacefully and ended in mayhem and full-on fighting. Hands were used, things were thrown and smashed; anything was used as a weapon. Barrack dwellers cowered in fear, praying windows and doors stayed intact in the aftermath. Concerned loved ones rushed out to assist injured partners or friends and assess damaged property. The smell of alcohol, from empty or full bottles thrown during the fight, and dried drops of blood were covered with dry sand. Cops held off drunk drugged and belligerent men, as interfering relatives pleaded for leniency from the police while screaming at the unruly mob to behave. We watched from behind our closed windows in fascination and horror as the spectacle unfolded. Cops sped away with a van full of drunken louts as stones rained down on the government cars, their dogs barking furiously until they disappeared out of sight. The strange quietness after the storm was just as unsettling as tried to get some sleep, hoping the captured men would be taught a lesson.

Sadly, no jail cell held them for a long period, and they returned madder than before. The fear they instilled in the area was palpable as once carefree neighbours took refuge in their homes, windows shut, and doors bolted shut. Open happy friendships dwindled in the face of distrust, mistrust or paranoia after the arrival of police in the area. They accused innocent people of being informers and snitches to gain favour with the cops.

Close friends and once happy neighbours became enemies, embroiled in petty fights which led to a mass shout out of name calling and accusations. The mere mention of a name instilled fear in people and intimidation became another threat to our friendly co-existence. The weak, mild, shy and timid were preyed on, and gangs picked on those who "needed to be taught a lesson'" over some slight, imagined or not. Until there was a trail of blood on the ground, no one took a back seat. Sirens, barking dogs or gunshots we took for granted, instilled panic at most, but nothing was as fearsome as the flick of the small knife carried by most gangsters. The okapi replaced the crude broken bottle neck stabbing device which led to much more bloodshed on our sandy pathways and tarred roads.

These lock-back or slip-joint knives were made around 1902 and sent to the German colonies in Africa. Named after the central African animal okapi, used by poor people for their everyday use, until it became a status symbol and nicknamed "Saturday night special" of knives. Gangsters sat around cleaning and polishing their okapis and held "flicking" contests to see who could draw a knife the fastest.

The small flick knife became way too small for the cowards, so they improvised with a machete or panga, hoping to inflict many wounds and as much damage as possible. They had little or no sympathy over the pain and destruction wrought upon people or property. Being a scarred, tattooed jailbird survivor increased their street credentials as much as the intimidation factor. All we did was grin and bear the slow decline of our once clean and harmonious patch of low roofed homes.

Gangs increased their stranglehold of fear as much as parents guarded over kids and a targeted, malleable or easily influenced family member. Warned to avoid any contact or interaction without annihilating them, kids were used to collect or carry a wrapped parcel, no questions asked. We knew not to tell cops or parents about being mules and to hide and spend the compensation without raising suspicion.

They made everything look exciting except when it came to the fights, bloodshed and police raids. Some residents tried to maintain a bit of respect and decency around the barracks, but they were being outnumbered by the sheer prosperity favouring the bad people around the place. It seemed crime and criminal activity did pay.

The absurdity of the situation was lost as they all smoked, drank, danced, laughed and sat together before proceeding to kill, maim or fight one another. Yet bring in the cops and they all stood as one to protect each other. This was confusing since cops were on hand to remove troublemakers, yet we stood united to protect our hardened gangsters.

As cops flung people into their vans, relatives retaliated by dragging them back out as we watched the circus unfold on a regular basis. The cops were 'hearing dust'—slang for taking no nonsense and did their job.

Restoration to walls, windows, doors, fences, faces and other body parts ensued until the next skirmish. Kids walked around picking up fallen change or "magically" found a few coins hidden earlier and spent with others to avoid arousing any suspicions. With a bunch of bad role models, what did you expect to happen? Praised and lauded as we misdirected the 'gattas' —nickname for the cops—we were just as guilty. The wrath of a gangster or his henchman struck with little or no mercy. While cops reinforced their presence with batons and canines, the cocksure gangsters, drug dealers, their cohorts and clients, hopped in and out of the detention cells with poise and nonchalance.

The barracks had become a hotbed of criminal activity and violent confrontations in less than two years. An unseen dark cloud and pervading sense of unease filled the air, as adults looked for ways to deal with or handle some of the issues. Sadly, for one little boy, the barracks would become an unhappier and miserable place.

Chapter 10: collingwood primary school and scholastic scrapes

Having turned six late in 1973, I started school in January 1974. A vague memory of getting dressed in a white shirt, short grey pants and socks, not sure if the outfit was brand new or second-hand, I was taken to my first school. We arrived at the school gates and joined a throng of distressed kids, worried parents and smartly dressed men and women bustling around us. These were the teachers who would look after us for a few hours a day. Even though we had been prepared for this day, the reality was very daunting as we waited for proceedings to start. Remember, pre-school classes were an alien concept in my coloured community at the time.

Exasperated parents reminding kids they "could not wait for them to start school" just to have some peace and quiet around the home, may have impacted on the distressing scenes outside the school gates. Teachers asked our names, wrote them down and pinned a piece of paper on our chests. Cries turned to sniffles as the sun glinted off our shiny faces, arms, legs and gleaming hair smeared with Vaseline, the body lotion of the poor masses.

Put into groups, kids sharing a first name were evenly spread among the ranks, while some mothers insisted their kids be in a specific teacher's class, allowed for some lighthearted bickering until order was restored. Disgruntled parents left with their kids and told to bring us back the next day for our first real day at school. Despite the tantrums and tears, I joined one of many Sub A classes of 1974 at my very first primary school, Collingwood.

Once I entered the school gates for the second time, everything became blurred, hazy and vaguely blank. Yet another conundrum I faced when writing was that the first two years of my schooling career were foggy and remain a near mystery to me. Drawing a blank as much as I tried to regress, the idea of a hypnotist crossed my mind. Told that not many hypnotists were happy to retrieve years of suppressed memories, I decided to leave the sleeping dog alone. My recollection before and after the first two years at school are vivid; the perplexing vacuum is bothersome to say the least.

For the first two years, they taught us the basic skills to read, write, count and how to use our fine motor skills for everyday living. We got to draw childish sketches, build things with small wooden blocks and play games in and out of the classroom, getting to know different colours, shapes, sizes and the important rules for the next twelve or so years of school. Not all the time would be spent behind a desk, fortunately. There would be days for proper sports, games and festivities with other schools in the area. Joining my two older siblings at the same school, every parent expected their child to go the distance and finish their education before the age of 18.

Elder siblings dragged their smaller relatives along meandering litter-lined paths and roads to school. Straggling kids played games and pranks until they learned that being late was not an option. News got back to parents about any bad manners and there would be hell to pay, never mind the public humiliation and teasing for being told off in front of your peers. Being naughty to some degree was fine but labelled as the 'teacher's pet' was not always a good thing. We were taught manners, calling teachers "Miss So and So" or "Sir This and That" at every turn and greeted everyone in the morning, afternoon and said goodbye when we left for home. Parents had their rest while teachers dented some manners, simple knowledge and rules into our little heads. Sometimes, parents were not always happy with some teaching or punishment methods, which provided a bit of light relief among corridors during the day.

Walking home after school was a different matter as we cut corners, taking short cuts through yards, scaling fences and looking for trouble. Hens incubating eggs under the hedges were always a target. Irate hens and owners chased after us, egg yolks littering escape routes. It meant a longer different route to school for a few weeks.

We beat the hens to hatching eggs but in class I was beaten for being slow at writing a few sums on the blackboard. For every mistake, the teacher rained down blows to the back of my legs with a ruler or cane. The pain panicked me, the shame paralyzed my brain as I went blank and let her whip me until someone else took my place. My long socks and thick coating of Vaseline on legs provided some protection, as did an extra pair of shorts under the grey school slacks. Our teacher wore a wig, so every now and again, someone tugged at it and we all suffered, but it was worth it. Pulling it right off was bonus points. She wore glasses, was very fair and we shall call her Mrs Jagger so as all names and descriptions are changed to protect and deter any libel letters coming my way.

Beatings in class were meant to strengthen our resolve to learn, with parents offering their opinion that perhaps we deserved it. Teachers hardly caned kids whose parents had no issue walking up to them, demanding answers when kids complained to them.

Kids from the barracks were either tough or their uneducated parents saw little wrong with some discipline since they meted out the same at home. I knew my parents got intimidated by authority figures, so chances of them facing a teacher were very slim.

Starting school, I noticed that some kids lived in bigger homes, had nicer clothes and brought better lunches to school. Our plain peanut butter and jam sandwiches paled in comparison and were eaten out of sight. Donated sandwiches were on offer to the less fortunate on most days— three cardboard boxes of brown bread covered in syrup, jam or peanut butter. Placed outside the office, an appointed teacher stood guard, dishing out hot soup on some days. Even in poverty, we were too proud to accept free meals or got teased as we made our way towards the bread and soup, shame overpowering the hunger pangs and growling in the belly.

The free sandwiches and soup went to waste on 'bunny chow' day at school. Begging poor parents to pay for a meal from our past, we waited impatiently for the knock on the door. Those without a curry bunny meal, begged, hassled or snatched and ran. The walk of shame to the big brown boxes was the other option.

A girl in class, Flora, always had tasty packed lunches in her school desk. Polony was a treat in a few homes, while cheese was a rare delicacy to say the least. The much sought after tasty polony is said to be derived from mortadella, a finely ground pork sausage with cubes of pork fat, from the Italian city of Bologna. Other than pork. chicken, turkey, beef, venison or soy proteins could be added, while they added black pepper, nutmeg, allspice, celery seed and coriander to the original Bologna sausage.

So, when we spotted Flora's neatly wrapped lunch, it was no contest. They ate some or all of it, depending on her reaction. Kids, including myself, could so mean and cruel. We took our lunch home, in case there was nothing to eat or grabbed the free slices from school. This bread, coupled with a cup of sweet or weakened black tea, was the after school meal for many a kid from the barracks.

Bread slices got thinner and tea weaker as the days progressed in most homes, so the free bread from school came in handy at times. One never knew when the next thick slice of bread would show up on an enamel saucer, bearing in mind these were days before sliced bread came along. Flora was not the only girl who suffered in the class or school. A distant cousin, a girl called Sandra, had a habit of coming to school with or without knickers or not getting to the toilet on time. Kids followed, pulling, teasing and taunting and laughing at her. No one came to her rescue as we watched her get publicly shamed, scared to take on the bullies and face the same treatment. Mrs Jagger deserved our wrath for caning us, but we were unnecessarily cruel to Flora and Sandra. In the name of fun, we joined in bullying and teasing my cousin and a classmate, ignoring the misery we heaped onto them.

Besides Miss Jagger, Flora, Sandra, and another girl called Anita, I have no memory of any other person in my class. The bread in boxes, soup, 'bunny chow' days are also vivid recollections, yet amazingly I draw a blank at everything else. I know there were sports days, but only a vague memory of the large grassy patch behind the made school filled with screaming kids. Whether I was a spectator or mini athlete remains a mystery.

Those three girls are the only ones in my memory, and I find it very odd. Don't you? I jump into the future and the year 1988 and a chance meeting with a man called Tony. We met at a house party, he took one look at me, said he knew me as David when we shared a classroom in Collingwood primary school. Well, slap me with a feather, but I drew blanks at his name, face or the memory, Tony on the other hand had a very clear memory of what I had gone through.

That I might have had a best friend or no friend at all, and not recall, is sad. It is odd that I vividly recall my first shack home, its contents, then relocating to the brick house and the gang fights around us yet draw a complete blank about those first two years at school. Even stranger is that all this took place in a matter of four years. Very strange indeed.

There were no signs that I would suffer a fate much worse than my two classmates in later years. Karma, genetics or merely the unluckiest boy in the barracks at the time? Our earlier, fun-filled life in the barracks had morphed us into being scared and wary of the gangsters, drug lords and users. We made the most of trying to live around each other and everyone who passed through the barracks. It got notorious as being a place where angels fear to tread its shifting sands. While most residents appeared indifferent over the fights and parties, no one took notice of the older, curly-haired boy who joined in the fun and games with the other kids. He watched, circled and waited for the chance to pounce. When he did, the innocent prey and victim stood no chance at all.

Chapter 11: secretly, someone is watching over me

Somehow, the adults and kids accepted their daily grind, surviving in the barracks and I have a vague memory of belonging to a group of boys who played together. We played pranks, teased, imitating the fights and police raids around us. A normal bunch of little boys and I saw myself as part of the crowd, no different to any other boy, nor singled out for being odd at all. Boys were boys and girls were girls.

Clifton, one of my playmates, lived in the party house next door. His green eyes made him the darling of all adults while some kids envied him. Having a set of bright green or blue eyes, hair that bounced and flounced with every flick of your neck, placed one very high up in the popularity stakes.

Materialism had not reared its head yet since we were all poor, but kids knew what it meant to be blessed with good looks, straighter hair and coloured irises. That Clifton was precociously cute added to his charm, but his family home was the main source of all the partying and shenanigans. We allowed him to lead games and kept him happy in case he ran home and complained about us.

Despite the violence and criminal activity around the place, I was quite docile and not the sort to start a fight or get involved in physical scraps. Playful fights were the norm around little boys, while bruised egos, cowards and bullies a given. My parents being laid back, passive and non-violent, were unsettled by the constant fights and mayhem around us.

Too engrossed in being a little boy among friends, we had no idea a dark set of eyes watched us frolic in the sand, sun, or rain. Pitch black eyes trailed one boy, biding his time to make a move while the unsuspecting victim had no idea he was the target.

Chapter 12: an innocent prey, a small toy for a big boy

After school activities around the barracks were no different to any other day, weather dependent naturally. We played games, created new ones for amusement, the noise or

excited screams annoying those trying to rest. We played indoors, until noisy fights or arguments got us evicted. Adults looked out for those kids whose parents worked or ran errands since there was no after school care back in the 70's.

Harvey, a distant and older cousin, or so I was told, was fair, taller with curly hair and the owner of those black eyes. He was different or 'slow' and we learned he had some temper when things did not go his way. Game rules were changed as he disrupted and cheated or started arguments. Unlike Clifton, kids stood up to him, yet oblivious to his agenda, which had my name written all over it.

Over time, it became clear Harvey trailed me around the place, a lurking shadow over every game and move I made. Since he was my cousin, it did not seem a big deal and aware of his temper, we found his constant presence amusing and then unsettling. Of course, I had no description for his stalking and taking his attentiveness for granted. I became his special friend. Unsure how to deal with it, I let him dictate the game plan he had in store for me or us.

Harvey and I became peas in a pod. Cousins, though distant, a six-year gap in age and no one batted an eyelid at the friendship. When called out to play, I knew Harvey was behind it. Finding myself the mediator between a cheating Harvey and a pack of irate kids, I was promptly dragged away if they ganged up on him.

Our parents were always telling us 'to go play outside' for whatever reason and home owners were child friendly, until we overstayed or overplayed our welcome. With no big trees to climb, small patches of grass, teeming with rats and possibly snakes, gave us cover during our favourite game. Racing away to hide, I had no idea that a simple childish game of hide and seek would change the course of my life forever.

Read on, play catch up and decide if there were specific signs or perhaps destined for everything that came my way. This may shock those close to me, those who know or think they know what made into the adult I am today. Somebody may have suffered a similar fate, or you know someone who has, and the outcome might be different to my own. We might endure similar struggles and experiences, but no two persons may give an identical outcome. This story may be an emotional roller coaster of a ride, so I beg you to hold on tight for the next few paragraphs, pages and chapters.

Hide and seek ensured we passed a few hours as we hid behind doors, corners, under beds, behind or inside wardrobes and boxes. Excitable kids seeking hiding spaces did offer a welcome distraction from the monotony and daily routine in the barracks with the adults often joining in the fun as they kept watch or gave us away. Harvey on the other hand, took matters in his own hands and I had no reason not to follow his lead.

He took charge of our hiding spots, ignoring any other suggestions. We were counted out first or last or never at all. Whether the latter was deliberate because he was such a bully, we stayed hidden, sometimes ages after the game had ended. Whether he kept me at his side on purpose, I felt or found nothing odd or strange about it. Hiding areas or spaces became smaller and over time I realized my cousin wanted me right next to him, hidden from view and any prying eyes. Despite my not being happy with his choice in our hideouts, Harvey had no reason to force me into the tiny spaces. I merely felt I had to play along by some unknown force or feeling.

We progressed from standing, kneeling and sitting in the tiny spaces, finally crawling in to lie down and hide. I scrambled in and lay face down while he followed, gingerly settling over me as we both kept watch. Racing out to score was never going to occur and he had no intention of playing real hide and seek, except his version and nothing was going to stop him as he carefully laid out the ground rules. No puns intended.

Once Harvey had me conditioned and comfortable in our hiding place, he took an age to settle down on top of me. If sighted by the seeker, we stayed hidden, convinced he was out and I still in the game. Unsure and confused, I let him press me into the soft sand while I kept watch, though deep down I knew the game was over and our own private one had begun. There was no reason to push him off since I had no idea what he was doing to me. No matter how much I shifted to accommodate his body over mine, Harvey could not stop moving his bigger body over my own.

In the beginning, we whispered as we watched and listened, but once he fidgeted and crawled over me, an uneasy silence appeared. Not yet eight years old, the unease was replaced by faint discomfort that something was not quite right. Under his spell and a bit scared, I never called a halt to the proceedings or questioned his actions.

Assuming it was some game big boys played, I joined Harvey in the confined space as he wriggled and squirmed

103

over me, never asking whether I was happy to play along. That we had to be out of sight was another issue I hardly took into consideration and may I say, it did not have to be a game of hide and seek either. My older cousin sought me out and promptly dragged me away for his own private game. I offered little resistance while the other kids started to notice his odd behaviour.

Even though no one asked or spoke about our hiding arrangements, I felt other people knew what we were up to. Paranoid and nervous, I felt tense as Harvey watched over our games, waiting for a chance to drag me away. He disrupted games or dragged me away despite protests from others. Torn between fleeing or facing my fate, we glared at him for different reasons, eyes filled with pity and many with keen interest. No one saw the confusion and panic in my own. When he was a no show, I was relieved and if he ignored me during games, I felt hurt and shunned at the same time. On my own, I was a spare wheel, aware I could be carted off at any minute. Watching a game from the sidelines was no fun, as I played a game and watched it spiral out of control.

Somehow, we both knew a line had been crossed, still unsure which one or why and a deepening silence was proof of that. The other kids teased me, yet I had no idea what they were hinting at or implying. Harvey on the other hand got angry and chased after them as the confusion within me grew. Why was he aggressive over the teasing while I felt shy, awkward and perplexed that others felt the need to mock us for what we did when alone and hidden from view? Staying away or hiding from my persistent cousin was easier said than done, but I gave it a shot.

Harvey sent other kids to find me and they chanted my name until I was forced to go out and play. Other than the names I mention, I have no recollection of having a close friend, besides Harvey, who was not really a friend. Naturally all names are changed.

The kids took pleasure in dragging me to Harvey, handing me over like a sacrifice, as I tried to break free. Laughing at my discomfort, confusion and fear, I knew the game rules had changed and everyone had to know what he was doing to me. Feeling alone and trapped, their words and jeering echoed while I let Harvey lead away. Face down and fighting back the tears, I accepted the inevitable until it was time to slink back to our flat roofed house, dusting myself off as I went along.

Our hidden escapades were not much of a secret as time dragged along. Tucking my face into the crook of an arm, Harvey distracted with whatever he was doing, the sudden loud screaming voices made us both jump. The older boy scrambled out, giving chase while I curled into a ball. Feeling ashamed and embarrassment, I knew Harvey would not return. I had to face the music alone, aware that I was being called names for my friendship with him. After being found out, Harvey lay low and left me alone, but I was not exempt from the teasing and name calling. Initially, the taunts hardly made much of a mental impact. Harmless teasing by kids my own age, they said, yet no one was prepared for the damage and scars they would eventually create.

Harvey left me alone but stayed close, too scared to touch or drag me away. Our little secret was exposed, and it was only a matter of time before he started again. This time around, he had no reason to drag me away. I went along willingly.

Partly to avoid a scene and the taunts, which happened anyway and partly of some strange feeling that I wanted to go with this older boy. We were doing something naughty and yet I felt it was not bad at all. It was all very confusing as we rolled around, covered in grass and sand. The high sun and humidity allowed us to walk, run and play dressed only in our threadbare shorts and sometimes the odd vest.

An innocent game of hide and seek followed by one of cat and mouse, my shame and apprehension growing as Harvey upped the stakes. Undeterred when other kids found us, he waited until they got bored and left, keeping me prisoner while their hurtful words echoed in my head. Adults on the other hand saw two boys hiding, saw nothing amiss and walked away. My face hidden, they would never see the hurt and confusion or the quiet acceptance of what was happening to me.

I quietly welcomed the bigger body over mine as Harvey wriggled away and when I felt something hard press into my back, there was another shift in the air around us. I froze and unsure how to respond this new development, he stopped and I when I gave no resistance, he pushed himself harder against me. The soft soil giving way while he breathed near my ear. Without a saying a word, he crawled away, not bothered about the little boy he left in the sand. Scared and bewildered, I could not describe what had just happened, but I knew there was more to come. My dear cousin had lured me right into his game and we both knew I was not going to run or tell anyone.

The hours I spent at school allowed me freedom from Harvey or when the sun made way for a wet and rainy season. Hiding inside was the perfect excuse until the lure of playing, falling, sliding and pushing each other around in the mud became enticing. A few strategically placed pieces of wooden planks and cardboard saw us traverse along muddy terrain to run errands or get up to no good. Our lack of raincoats during heavy rains and treacherous paths were other reasons for skipping school. With only the tiny transistor radios for aural entertainment, we read or told stories, jokes, played snakes and ladders, other board and card games or made up new games as we went along.

Harvey put the rainy season to good use by getting me over to his house. Some adults worked while neighbours kept watch over the place and kids and since he was almost a teenager, he was a law unto himself. With only one door in and out of each home, it was a prison and no different to the tiny hiding spaces he used before. Behind a single closed door and drawn curtains, I was at his beck and call as he took full advantage of me. The odd knock at the door provided some respite but I was never going to flee or cry out. Completely under his spell, I found the hard thing pressing at me somewhat curious and bewildering, yet I never questioned, and he never explained. I did wonder if all boys played this game and whether he did it to the other boys as well.

Why was I chosen to be his playmate in this private and secret game? That I remained silent, offering little or no resistance, spoke volumes, while he mentally lulled me into submission. There was no need to use physical restraint. and no one noticed how his presence affected me. I was nervous before he made a move, and much quieter and composed after a 'special' game, masking the confusion, shame and guilt well. If other kids made an issue about it, I blanked them out, but their words hurt, creating a bit more confusion in my head and heart.

I was a small boy being used by my older cousin, making sure the other kids brought me to him when I tried to flee. They happily told other kids about me, the bully count increasing as much as my popularity. Every kid seemed to know about Harvey and me, yet no adult made any mention or asked me about the situation. Boys did not sleep on other boys at any time, did not allow it to happen, which meant there was something not right within me. Harvey was treating me like a girl but at no time did I feel like I was a girl, nor did I act like one. Of course, we knew about boyfriends and girlfriends, but I saw myself as one of the boys. Though around this time, I found myself relegated to the girls' team. They sought me out as a playmate and vice versa. The strange part was that Harvey kept his distance when I was among the girls. His actions confused me, so I found myself wrestling with more than I had bargained for.

Harvey had no issue facing up to anyone calling him names yet left me at the mercy of tormentors who ridiculed and mocked his smaller cousin. I found myself becoming silent and wary of anyone around the barracks, avoiding taunting kids and Harvey, but scared an adult might find out what we were doing.

My older deviant cousin watched my every move. Keeping a distance encouraged him to pursue, sweetening the capture and heightening my public humiliation. He paraded around like a marauding giant, yet I began to wilt under the scrutiny, name calling and bullying. At no time did anyone come to my rescue, making me feel even more alone and isolated.

Ignored by the others, I had no choice but to accept the advances and company of the boy who took me aside, placating his hormonal needs. I became his toy, something he touched, never considering my feelings. As time passed, he whisked me away and did not care if others followed us. Harvey rocked his body onto mine, oblivious that others looked at what he was doing. Their shouts and taunts did nothing to dampen his ardour. This was a new aspect to his grinding motions. Assured his docile gazelle would not flee, it was time to introduce the next phase of the game.

Despite all the fanfare around me, I felt very alone and dealt with the emotional turmoil as best I could. I never told anyone about the confusion about our friendship and how it affected me. Secretly enjoying the attention, I offered less resistance, even fooling a part of myself into thinking that Harvey was less aggressive towards me. Those early feelings of fear, shame, confusion and disgust were melting away and it puzzled me. I knew there was something wrong and bad about what we were doing, yet why did we continue, and I not put a stop to it? Partly afraid and not sure how to handle the mixed emotions, I looked out for him, accepting his misplaced affections for the need to feel loved, wanted and accepted. Alone with my cousin, I let him take the lead, afraid and unsure how to respond or behave. We knew he had a mental or a learning disability, and the mood swings unnerved me, so I kept quiet as he rocked and pushed his body down on my own. We had the routine worked out, no words ever passed between us, so when I heard him ask me to turn and face him, I was surprised but complied as expected.

Turning to look back at him, he shifted, telling me to roll over onto my back and once again, I did as he requested. Settling down over me and not missing a beat, he rocked his lower body against my own. Shy and unsure where to look or what to feel, I squeezed my eyes shut, waiting for the next cue, but I knew I was in trouble.

Memories flashed of a game we played before relocating to the barracks, dolly house, a game where kids get a chance to play at being grown up. At some point things got a bit hazy, there were screams and scenes as angry parents and adults dragged kids out of sight or home. Those not given a chance to explain until after the beating, someone found a boy and girl in a compromising position, too young to know what was wrong, but very disturbing, nonetheless. Perhaps this put me off girls for life. Just teasing, so I knew Harvey was using me as a mummy to his daddy, and we had to hide. Since we were boys, why hide even though the other boys knew what we did? No adult offered to find or beat us up over our game or friendship. Self-conscious and afraid, I was too aware my cousin had plenty more in store for me, himself and perhaps both of us.

On my way to school, kids mocked me. telling everyone what Harvey and I did when we were hiding or alone. They said I was his girlfriend. Kids peered and stared at me, others brave enough to joke and tease, expecting a physical or verbal response. I gave none, but Harvey chased them down. Once the novelty wore off, they left us alone, but the odd comment did not go amiss. We made light of them, including myself, putting it down to childish games and pranks. Boys were good at being boys, except we were the only two doing it around the barracks.

Sadly, not everyone was relaxed about our boy-on-boy antics. It was wrong and since I allowed it to happen, something must be wrong, with me and not him. No one blamed the older boy for using me to satisfy his adolescent needs. Initially, I followed blindly as led me away until we were found out. Then he toyed with me, using others to hand me over like a sacrifice, pretending it was a little game. I was totally under his control and found myself waiting for him to make a move towards me. My emotions were all over the place, my head cried out for freedom from his clutches while I wanted to feel my cousin lie over me. Scared yet excited, I had no idea when the feelings started and why I felt that way over someone who never thought about my feelings at all. We had no idea my daily misery was about to multiply in spades.

The new name followed my every move and if any adult heard, no one questioned the baying kids around me. Racing away to hide, they chased while I covered my ears to drown out their words. Tiny hands grabbed at my own to make sure they were heard. I never fought them off or cried until they got bored and left, disappointed but vowing to never let me forget I was doing something bad with another boy. There was a word for it, yet nothing registered through the maze of taunts. I was learning at a young age to shut down out mentally and they had no idea how deep their words would hurt and affect me in the future. For now, we called it child's play.

Nothing Harvey did to me was child's play. He now had me lie flat on my back while he lay down over me and moved around. Closing my eyes provided an escape as I felt him look down at me. With no warning, I felt his lips on my neck and jumped at the odd sensation. What was he doing, but he kept his face pressed into my neck, hardly moving until he felt me relax and not try to escape, and then he ran his lips over my neck. My heart raced as Harvey rocked with his lips tracing my exposed neck as I pondered his excitement while I felt a deep sense of sadness mingled with guilt.

As I got used to his lips on my neck, he added another element of surprise. Taking my smaller hand, he pressed it against the front of his shorts. I knew it was wrong and did try to pull my hand away, but he was having none of it. Nothing felt right and we both knew it as I let him use my hand to do as he pleased. Despite not undressing, that odd feeling of being dirty and soiled lingered as he ran off. My whole body flushed with a childish wonder that he may have other instalments to add soon.

Perhaps now that we had both settled into the game, he was in a hurry to lead the way and educate his little docile cousin. The rocking body motion continued as lips played with the skin of my neck before settling over my own. Opening my mouth in protest, instead, I felt our tongues touch, and this time I tried pushing him off me. He stopped kissing me but kept me pinned under him until I relaxed. Promising not to do it again, he moved his lips closer while I vigorously shook my head from side to side. Both boys knew another milestone had been reached, with the younger one feeling excited yet confused about kissing another boy and enjoying the feeling. It was my very own secret, a pleasure I could share with no one else.

Powerless to break his hold over me or my silent acceptance of his special attention, I relented and gave him free rein over my clothed body, neck and lips. Fighting a deep yet unsettling need to lie down under Harvey, we knew the score once alone. While it appeared not to bother him that I was a boy, I never questioned why I was singled out to be his 'girlfriend' and allow him to stick his tongue in my mouth. Kids naming and shaming me around the place, did nothing but make my day miserable and sometimes unbearable.

The social isolation and almost constant hinting at my depraved actions, sent me into the arms of the one person I despised yet needed. Wrestled, licked, kissed and pawed at by Harvey, I was either shunned or pulled, chased and teased around the place. Not sure if I was a leper or plaything from one day to the other, no one saw the confusion, pain, sadness and panic in my eyes. The emotions excited Harvey but I stored them in a dark space in my head and heart. We were oblivious to the fact that a few boys were waiting for the right time to make their move and pounce.

Chapter 13: a tattered friendship tests brotherly love

Among the many brown-coloured kids, Stiena with her pale skin, blonde hair, and fluent Afrikaans, was an oddity. We played together, and I had no problem understanding my friend since it was my mother's main means of communication. I had little idea that Afrikaans and a Durbanite were never mentioned in the same sentence. So, we were a cut above the rest with the three languages spoken in our household. Not that any of us kids spoke it or any Zulu and Xhosa anyway. While I tested my verbal aerobics on Stiena around the barracks, Harvey kept his eye on me. Never in a million years did I expect his next move.

Isolated and brainwashed into going with him, he assumed my friendship with Stiena would be a walkover for the next stage of his game. Enticing us to play in the house, I was not sure how to deal with having a real girl, or another person for that matter, be a witness to my shame. Resisting his advances, afraid she would run and tell on us, we seemed to be wrestling playfully, so she saw no reason to leave the room. I was intent to keep him off me so after a while and without warning, Harvey turned and lunged at her.

Though timid and soft spoken, she was no pushover or happy to wrestle with any boy and promptly screamed at the top of her lungs. The noise brought adults rushing in to investigate, finding two scared kids and a shocked older boy. Confusion ensued as we were dragged out, Stiena to safety while I got the second best beating of my life. Both scared of Harvey, I was blamed for getting her into the room in the first place and warned to stay away from the older boy with mental issues. No one knew the rest of the story or mentioned my predicament. Though the story faded, the stigma surrounding Harvey lingered, and no one dealt with the incident or took notice of the docile little victim at the centre of it all.

He left me alone and I kept my distance, the freedom and respite from his advances a blessing. I got blamed for his disturbed behaviour as the teasing escalated around me. Nicknames, horrible words and taunts were darted at me during the day while I crept into the single bed, scared yet defiantly fighting back the tears. I hurt all over with no idea where it hurt the most. It appeared everyone called me something terrible and no one wanted to be around me, except Harvey.

Hiding forever was never an option so I gingerly ventured out to face Harvey, hordes of kids happy to tease and shame me for being another boy's girlfriend. I wondered if he roped in other kids for his private game while I was unavailable, but I was the only one facing the firing line for doing something wrong. Confused over his attention and my acceptance of everything we did, at no time did I think of myself as being anything but another little boy, despite references around the place to my being treated like a girl. I became known for being different, not in the same vein as my older cousin, though, who had no idea his hold over me was about to be challenged.

Once the Stiena episode died down, it was only a matter of time before Harvey would drag me aside and continue where he left off. Well, drag may not be the best word at this point, as I secretly wished he would have sought me out again. I could not explain these deep strange feelings I felt at the thought of being held by him. What started out as a game for him was turning into something very different for me, yet I gave nothing away. He appeared in control, and I was not going to burst his bubble. Mentally and emotionally I may have jumped ahead of those around me, but with no close friend, I kept this all to myself.

Most kids, or other boys, knew or had some idea what Harvey and I got up to, so there was little surprise when Clifton, the green-eyed terror, joined me in a hiding spot. We were of similar age and it seemed he came with some experience. Feigning surprise at his presence, I was rolled onto my back and he shifted his body over mine. Making it seem like the most natural thing to do, my friend placed his lips over my own and did something I felt was ever so right. My cauldron of mixed emotions felt ready to burst from our childlike display of physical affection.

Clifton clearly knew how to kiss another boy. I never questioned the how and why, so he took liberties whenever he felt the need. I had two boys chasing me, and of course I chose Clifton over the older, rougher Harvey. Everything felt so right in my head and heart, which eased the pain of being ridiculed and mocked. Reliving the kisses on my neck and lips helped ease the emotional torture, torment and pain.

First Harvey, then Clifton, and before they knew it, there was a rotating wheel of boys sniffing around me, the game of hide and seek merely a front as they led me away. It appeared Harvey had done his homework, preparing me for the next phase of my own temperamental growth. Accustomed to another boy's body close to mine, childish lips kissing my own, the urge to resist and fight had almost evaporated. If I did, it was just a formality in case another kid happened to find us in a compromising position. Boys found it funny when caught, joining the crowds to verbally pelt me with names while I cowered in shame and bewilderment. Why was I being made the scapegoat over our boyish dalliances?

Two became three, four, five, until I lost count, being the constant in the equation and allowed them to take advantage and tag me as a girlfriend. Externally I was indignant, while rejoicing internally at the prospect of being liked by more than one boy. We had overstepped the friendship boundary, and my social status was clear to all and sundry. Not every boy was happy to go public about kissing another boy, so we ducked and dived out of sight.

The leader, usually Clifton, gave a signal and I was led to a hiding place and then boy after boy had their way with me. My lips stung, cheeks and neck flushed from crude kisses and bites while I fought the urge to spit. I went from being a girlfriend to the resident courtesan and concubine in a short space of time. Bickering if a boy took his time or their turn in the line, I never saw them race away, ashamed or embarrassed over their actions. No one asked or explained why I was the target in the game of kiss and run. Invading my personal and private space, I was merely a body to curb an urge without a care for my own physical and mental needs.

The many boyish faces, lips, bodies, skin textures blended into one dark brown haze on top of me. I had no reason to say no to any boy who separated me from a group or game and led me away while his friends teased or cheered. Afraid to fall deeper into something others found repulsive, and fighting down the urges Harvey cultivated, I let them decide my fate. To this day, except Harvey and Clifton, every other boy who led me aside is a blank face and name. Physically and mentally engraved in my brain, it's difficult to forget their silent kissing, touching and fondling, nervous

117

breathing filling the air as they hurried to finish whatever they were doing. Shy, awkward and scared I would do something wrong, I left them in charge to direct and move my pliant body. I had only ever touched Harvey's private parts. The others were happy to kiss and run, so I became the poster boy or girl for those hoping to hone their kissing skills, and I wore my imaginary badge with pride despite being ostracized by some of my peers.

The very boys who kissed and fondled my body, joined in the masses to stone—not in the literal sense of course—and berate me in public. No one knew how badly I wanted to wrap my arms around each boy or my need to be hugged close. It felt so right, but I was too scared to make things worse and had no idea why I had the feelings. They did it for a laugh, but I knew it was what I wanted, and this scared me too. Was this meant to be, or was this a phase my friends and I were merely going through?

The switch from feeling cornered, hunted and used to being wanted, kissed and used, instilled a different mental perspective of my situation and status among other kids. It was a huge mental step to accept, yet not publicly acknowledge I was different to my other boyhood friends. There was a term for the type of person I would become, but I had to settle for the crude one for now. I was a moffie, a crude word for a boy or man regarded as effeminate. No one told me I was born to be a man of the earth, as nature, Harvey, Clifton, his cronies, or nurture had other plans for me. Persecuted publicly as they used me in secret, I remained silent and stoic, dealing with my personal internal battles as best an eight-year-old could.

At least two years had passed since Harvey took me aside and the other boys took it a step further. Whether they had been skilled at kissing was a point no one raised, but they bickered over who had the best technique as they watched each other kiss me. Hands held me down when I resisted and to anyone passing by, all they saw were a bunch of scruffy boys rolling about in the long grass and sand. Bite marks and bruises were too easily explained away as a rough game or play fight.

The physical mishandling and verbal catcalling created emotional angst about who or what I really was. I saw a little boy in the mirror; others saw and treated me like a girl on the playground. Confused and with no clear knowledge of when it had all changed for me, subconsciously I had accepted I was not going to be like the other boys. I was one of the girls during games and play yet switched sides when it suited the leader. It was also fine when a boy pushed or pulled me aside. I never resisted. Negative, nasty and hurtful comments floated around me and I realized kids could be horrible to each other from an early age. The ugly term 'bullying' had not reared its distasteful head yet.

The odd one out is always going to be the centre of attention, and kids got teased over things they had little or no control over. Whenever I left my front door, I was targeted by boys or bullies, and I was about to reach a turning point in my life as a known sissy boy on the block.

Mentally, I am almost at a loss of my time spent indoors with my family. I slunk into the small house, bathed and crept into bed without much of a fanfare, hoping my face or neck were free of our secret activities. Sharing a bed with my brother or father in a tiny room called for skillful cover ups. My family had no idea what I got up to, or so I assumed as no one spoke of me being a sissy or behaving like a girl. They never saw me navigate a path to and from school, dodging groups of teasing kids. I was the Pied Piper of the barracks, except I had a pack of dusty, mostly barefoot bullies around and behind me.

Different routes were useless; it only invited fresh tormentors while racing ahead and lagging had the same effect. Dashing home one day, I heard a voice call out to me and saw an old man standing in a doorway. He held out a hand, which I assumed held a sweet, and told me to come and get it.

Always told to be polite to older people, not to mention greedy for sweets, I stepped forwards but saw him turn and walk into the house, expecting me to follow. Unsure, I waited, not wanting to appear disrespectful or miss a free sweet. I stopped at the door and peered inside. He looked as old as my dad did, but everyone was ancient to a kid of my age. Waiting on the small concrete steps, I saw him sit on the couch and asked me to enter. I obeyed. Music and voices carried through the open doors and windows while I took stock of a house so different from ours. It was bigger with nicer furniture and expensive-looking ornaments and pictures. The man looked at me and back to the open door, took my small hand in his larger one and pulled me towards him. I found myself sprawled over his lap and it appeared as if he was about to spank my bottom.

Images of stealing chicken eggs and angry owners flashed in my mind as I tensed for his hand and the sting on my bum. I fell for the oldest trick in the book and was about to pay for it. Holding me tightly, he tucked one hand under my short grey pants and I felt him touch my bottom. Expecting a few painful slaps, I realized his hand was only rubbing my bare skin. Accustomed to smaller hands on my bare skin, this felt strange, so I froze, but he never stopped what he was doing.

I began to squirm in fear, shame filling my heart that he knew my secret. He told me to keep still but I had no intention of finding out what he had in store for me.

I relaxed as he rubbed my small bottom under the school shorts and I hoped that was all he wanted to do. When he tried pulling down my shorts, I was having none of that, and struggled until he let me go and I ran out the door. Shaken, scared and ashamed, I told no one about the incident but it heightened my senses around adult men. Boys my own age were easier to handle, even if they came in packs or groups. The old man did always wait at the door, calling my name, but I ignored him, those walking nearby eager to know what was going on. Guilt-ridden, I refused to explain, using different routes to avoid him. Aware I had been exposed to a bigger danger, I still stayed silent.

Was it possible my parents and siblings knew of my reputation yet ignored broaching the subject? The tormentors darted loud verbal assaults for maximum benefit at every corner, so they must have heard for sure. Unfortunately, what happened next created a huge emotional divide between blood brothers, pushing me into an even deeper pit of social isolation under my own roof.

As the light faded one evening, Harvey took me aside but instead of a hiding place, I was dragged around the corner and pushed down onto my belly. Weak light from the candles and paraffin lamps created dim shadows around us. Attuned to everyone's so-called daily or nightly routine, we would spot loiterers before they saw us in the semi-darkness. This time, however, Harvey changed his regime and pushed me on all fours and knelt behind me. Fully clothed, he began to push himself against me and all I had to do was play watchman for him. I had a vague idea of his actions but was too scared to tell him to stop or make a noise. We were doing something bad and my head whipped in all directions as I watched and prayed no one saw us.

Harvey got carried away and before we knew it, a voice demanded to know what we were up to, although it was obvious to all and sundry. Down on my knees, I could not get up fast enough as Harvey took off and left me to face the music and the owner of the familiar voice on my own. Shivering in the semi-darkness, I heard the angry voice, but his words were lost as I hung my head in shame and humiliation. My little body tensed in fear, but there was no need. I watched his shadow move and walk by as I lay down in the sand. I felt his disgust and anger and begged the earth to create a huge sinkhole for me. My older brother Frank had found me with another boy, acting like dogs and his little brother a very willing participant. My degradation was almost complete, with no idea the repercussion of being found out would be a much harder pill to swallow as I got up, slowly dragging my feet to our front door.

Frank was only three years older, yet I felt like a toddler entering the house, not sure if he exposed my shameful secret. I felt or imagined his eyes watching me, filled with a mixture of disgust and revulsion. Nervous and skittish, expecting the belt to appear any minute, I relaxed when nothing happened, grateful he had stayed silent yet sadly unaware of the long-term effect. Emotionally I had lost a brother in every sense of the word. His silence had effectively shut the door on exposing my misery over the last two or so years. There was no physical pain, so no tears were shed, which might have eased the tension I felt. After bathing, I quietly crept into bed and curled into a ball at the foot end, close to my father's feet, fighting down the urge to cry. Before the age of eight, I would never share a bed with my older brother again, banished to the foot end of my dad's bed. Frank became a silent figure around the house, making me feel I was to blame, my presence a daily reminder of the shame of having a sissy as a brother. A topic or subject never to surface, swept under the shiny linoleum forever.

In my tiny head and heart, I imagined he lost all respect for me. It was the last time Harvey would lay a finger or hand on me. It had come at a brotherly price, if not too late as well. I had paid dearly. Frank slowly froze me out, annoyed or irritated as I wilted into a smaller shadow of myself. The tiny home shrunk as I struggled with my inner demons. I was skittish and tense around him. Our physical and verbal interactions were strained, yet nobody noticed the shift in our behaviours or mentioned it. Frank, a bright older brother, slowly drifted away from me and over time, I watched him become a virtual stranger before my eyes.

Labelled by my playmates and bullies, yet secretly enjoying the attention I got from a group of boys my own age, I relaxed into the idea of being the token sissy or gay boy. My brother had found out, cutting me off in the process and, along with many others, disrespected my actions or behaviour. Some chose to make every single minute of my day a misery. Ostracized, I faced the minutes, hours, days, weeks and months with the quiet resilience and demeanour I had invented to protect myself. I vowed never to let a soul see me cry or break down, unwittingly adding veneers over mental and emotional freedom I may have enjoyed. Choosing to stay silent, with no better option back then,

I could not understand why I was I different or why no one liked me, deciding to pick and mock me instead. There were no external abnormalities; I was a mess inside and I could

123

not help the fact nor was I going to turn back time. Basking in a society hell-bent on engraving deep emotional and mental scars, no one told me of the painful and long journey I would still have to undertake before finding a cavernous sense of happiness and an almost lacklustre acceptance. David, the small bullied gay boy who would age and become an adult homosexual man, saturated with self-doubt, low self-esteem and a lack of confidence.

Chapter 14: blood brothers, a definite split in time

Harvey was finally out of the picture, yet my life's path had been altered and there was no turning back – a nurtured or naturally predestined conclusion. I was ignored by the boy who started it all, but now had Clifton and his posse to contend with. Physically one of the boys, it was noted I began to act and play like a girl. Shock and horror! Boys I met expected a passive, docile, submissive and non-threatening sissy, and the girls were indifferent to my status as their quasi-friend and confidant. The struggle to feel part of the group and be accepted raged as I was shunted between the opposing sides. One minute I had to behave like a girl as they kissed and fondled me, the next I had to be a boy and think like a girl to be included in a team. Bulldozed into these fractured mind games, I found myself absorbing a mentality contrary to my external attributes. Sadly, and unfortunately, I became my own role model and mentor, surrounded by gangsters I feared and the boys I liked, but who used me.

Except Terence. He had the darkest, smoothest skin I had ever seen, and he never took me aside. He was quiet and soft spoken, and we often played together. But this time I became a bully. When he refused to play by my rules, I retaliated by pinching him, racing away as he cried, but we always made up. Perhaps he felt sorry for me while I used him to vent a lot of my pain, anger and confusion.

While my own brother kept his distance, every other kid laid their hands, lips or body on me. There was a constant flow of tormentors, suitors or older men trying to cajole me into coming closer. A persistent presence throughout the day, trailing kids blocked my path when I ventured out. One day, they suddenly fled in all directions, despite no physical or verbal reaction from me. I looked up and saw my older brother walking in our direction. Fearing his response, I may have warned them not to bother as he never altered the pattern of his stride or glanced in our direction. Everyone watched the silent figure pass by, almost shocked at his indifference.

"Your brother is a sissy," some brave voice screamed after him, but he never stopped or turned in my defense. They goaded his retreating back as waves of humiliation and abject sorrow swept over me. My own flesh and blood sibling hated me enough to let the baying crowds vent their distaste for being different and girly. The maelstrom of activity around my family and me, Harvey and his game, Clifton with his troop, my first two years at school, our neighbours and colourful histrionics of life in the barracks, would be cemented, blurred, forgotten or erased from memory as the years passed. Of the two and a half years spent in the barracks, it is strange I have very little recollection of my time during actual school hours. Three girls from my class, the names of the boys I mentioned and the two very different families living amongst us, are the only solid memories I have from around that time.

Whatever I did outside the classroom while at school, is an absolute blank. Was there a reason for this? Yes, I tormented my brain over the many years of editing yet come up with zero answers. After almost twenty years away from the barracks, I visited the place and found Terence all grown up and living in the same house. We stared at each other like virtual strangers, his skin still as dark as ever. He had somehow survived, if not escaped the curse of the barracks, maturing into a young man, father and husband. Sadly, not every boy reached adulthood, I was informed. Drug use and the gang life had claimed the lives of names and faces I had forgotten or erased from memory. Bad or unfortunate choices left many families bereft of sons, husbands and daughters, not to mention a lifetime of pain.

If Harvey had not laid eyes and hands on me, would I too have become a young man, perhaps a father and husband like Terence, or had I been bundled along the righteous walkway of my life. As much as I tried to recall the other boys, nothing worked. All I came up with was Harvey, the main man, Clifton and Terence. The blanks bother me, and still do because I considered seeing a hypnotist. Advised to let sleeping dogs rest and slumber, I let the issue go. Sometimes the past is best left unearthed for a reason, and the results may not be suitable enough to digest. After rewinding and regressing a bit, let me draw you back to my past as it happened. Once again, I had no idea things were going to change and my time in the tiny brick house was coming to an end.

Chapter 15: a surprising removal and rushed relocation

I started a third school term, or Standard One, in 1975, aged 8 after relocating from a large ramshackle shanty home to a flat-roofed brick house with running water, lights and the hope of a fresh new start. The birth of gang culture and drug use provided a daily dose of conflict, dramatic parties and fights, yet a sense of camaraderie suffused the barracks. We looked out for one another, yet no one appeared to worry about me. I was daily fodder for those intent on making me suffer, my feeling and action dictated by those around me. Included one minute, then rudely rejected and ostracized, no one cared about my happiness. I braved feelings of loneliness despite having many people around me at any given time. Adept at withdrawing physically and emotionally, there was not much I could do about the verbal assaults, providing fodder for the future.

Running away to hide, only to be followed by a boy or a group, I started to encourage my suitors, maintaining the facade and not revealing my hidden feelings. When I was held and kissed, it was easy to shut out the misery and pain. Deep down I felt the joke was on them since I did like the boys kissing me, and no amount of teasing or bullying would change that. Wearing imaginary blinkers, I ignored comments and screams and gave little or no eye contact as I passed. Staring straight ahead or down at the ground, I maintained my stiff upper lip, combined with a purposeful strut and blank stare.

Maintaining my purposeful strut on the soft soil, filth-lined pathways and dusty roads was not easy, but I did my best, trailing crowds cursing and swearing in my wake. No one was going to get a response, verbal or physical, out of me. I was not programmed to be aggressive. Harvey and the other boys had trained me well. Submissiveness was a trait I adopted and when rumours circled about a possible change of homes, I gave a tiny prayer they were not true. We had just arrived and might be moved again. Where to and why? We had witnessed others come and go, but this time it would be our turn.

The rainbow chicken homes had become a hell hole for sure, but we liked living with the colourful residents, characters and friends. Their antics and my own escapades did make up a huge part of our daily lives. I might miss all this and perhaps it would be for the best. So, I waited for the rumours to become a reality.

My siblings and I were halfway into the school year, so moving sounded exciting yet daunting at the same time. A new home and school. Would I fit in, make a brand-new start, or face a new set of boys, older men and bullies? I learned to cope and face one day at a time, and I prayed we would stay in Wentworth. Alas, when a parade of uncles and aunts and relatives popped in, talks got underway, as was part of the culture to dissect and discuss the pros and cons. They decided we were to be moved to heaven knows where, the kids having no say in the matter. Informed that a new school, house, friends and relatives awaited us, there was no reason to prepare for the upcoming school exams.

Once again, the Calverley household packed their meagre belongings for the trip and to start a new life elsewhere, leaving relatives, old friends, in my case boyfriends and many bullies, behind. Very little details about the planning and execution of the move were made public until it was time to leave for the journey. The trip would take many hours and there was a strong possibility of never returning.

That I might not see my boyfriends, friends and bullies ever again, filled me with fear and a sense of freedom from all that I had been going through for the past three years.

Since my parents were unemployed, I saw no reason why we had to move in the first place. We had a real home, the barracks had turned bad, but we were happy, to say the least, and comfortable, or so it seemed. Perhaps they were looking to raise us in a better social setting and for the first time, I became the centre of attention for a very different reason. The sissy was leaving the rainbow chickens.

My mother was not happy about the long trek, while we looked forward to starting the journey and perhaps a better life in a new place, despite not being told where the new home was located. Relatives piled on the pressure with encouraging words, wishing it was them instead of us, my father answering questions with a silent authority. A fresh new school, home, friends and relatives awaited us on the other side, so we had to get out as soon as possible. It was no big deal, they said, so we took their word and got all our ducks in a row for the move, excited yet nervous about the adventure.

The news spread, and we packed in earnest. Well-wishers and scavengers popped into our home daily, staking claim to items we would leave behind. It would be a single trip and with few vehicles at hand, heavier items had to be sold or donated. A stack of flimsy cases, cardboard boxes and plastic bags was used for the bulk of our worldly goods. Poor as church mice, we owned a hand-carved wooden just, or chest. I had no idea where it came from, standing shiny and majestic in our dining room. My mom kept it polished and used it to store just about everything. Heartbroken and sad, we had to leave it behind, and I often wondered who took possession of that gorgeous wooden box. I would never lay eyes on it again. Fighting back the tears and mild fears over some things, we prepared to leave Duranta Road, Wentworth.

On the morning of departure, we loaded vans and cars with goods, saying goodbye to neighbours in the semi-darkness. Some were sad to see us leave, while I would miss a few of my friends, but not the bullies. We had over twelve hours of travel to cover, so once all our luggage and baggage were snugly tied into place, friends waved goodbye as the kombi full of adults and kids disappeared. My siblings and I had no idea what awaited on the other side.

The kombi, known as a bus or camper, was the type of panel van owned by most people in South Africa, useful for long trips, big enough to carry heavy items. It could carry many passengers, thanks to the adjustable seats. Made by the German company Volkswagen in 1950, it was to become the hippie van, except that there were no hippies around my house and 'hood.

Leaving the soot and grimy air behind us, our convoy sped along quiet roads, making a big deal about how great and necessary the move was for my family. It was a chance of a lifetime, though I'm not sure for whom precisely. There was no turning back. Cars sped on the highways, racing past huge grassy plains, hills and farmlands dotted with farms. We made short stops as we ate, refueled, refreshed and stretched our cramped bodies at a resting site.

Any doubts and questions were never voiced during our 407-mile trip to a seaside city called East London. Told that many excited relatives and friends awaited us, I had no idea whom they were talking about. I met my cousins once a year during the farm visits and had no idea which friends they were talking about. Anyway, the boiling sun and high humidity made the trip almost unbearable. We arrived in East London after sunset, all sweaty and irritable, yet excited it was over. The darkness made it impossible to compose any first impressions of the area, which I understood would become the new adopted hometown for us. We were here to stay for a very long time. I was totally unaware of what waited in the wings and hoped that history would not repeat itself. Well, I will let you be the judge.

Chapter 16: another tiny shack to my disjointed system

A weary bunch of drivers and travellers alighted, barking dogs and people bustled all around us, some welcoming and other staring at the new strangers. A normal-looking house stood in the yard, surrounded by a row of shacks at the back with a smaller free-standing one on the side. We watched strangers unpack and offload our essentials and dump them on the ground. Strange English and Afrikaans accents floated in the air as some swore and shouted at each other in jest. Inquisitive voices questioned in the dim light as kids rushed about excitedly, eager to carry and settle us in for the night.

Our minimal goods consisted of the two single beds, plain foam mattresses and a tiny wardrobe. Threadbare clothing, crockery, cutlery, paraffin lamps, cheap cooking and kitchen utensils made up the rest of our minimal luggage. It was not enough to fill the huge house with bright lights outshining the dim glow of candles and lamps from the shacks around it. Unsure what my parents were told, I saw helpers carry our stuff into a small shack at the back. Too tired to care, I assumed this a temporary sleeping place for the night. Using candle and lamplight, we prepared the beds and fell into a deep sleep, the rest of the stuff scattered on the floor. My dad and I curled up under the bed near the sole window of the shack, my sister and mother on the other, and my brother passed out on the thin foam mattress on the floor, snug between the two single beds.

At sunrise, we had a rude awakening. The shack walls and roof consisted of wooden planks or boards and strips of corrugated metal sheeting acting as a roof. My father, a tall man, almost touched the ceiling with his bald head, his stooped posture his saving grace. There was a single square window, and thin walls separated our shack from three others. Raised on a sandy bank behind the brick house, I thought someone was a joker and this was all one big prank.

Our stuff scattered around us, the shack looked even smaller, and where would we put everything? The shack was about the same size as the bedroom my dad, brother and I shared in Durban. Two adults, a teenager, an adolescent brother and myself, appeared disorientated and confused. Was this to be our new home? No one came around and it felt surreal. Unsure what to do, we sorted, packed and arranged our stuff and when no one came to explain the situation, reality sunk in very early. This was not close to the better option explained to us. We left a real brick house for a makeshift aluminium and plank box. Even our first shack was better than our newest home. There was no toilet, bathroom, kitchen or dining area, so how were we meant to live as we did before?

The shack felt like a prison cell, not that I had seen or entered one. Over the years, my living conditions would become something to be ashamed of, despite many families in the area living under the same circumstances. So, why was I unhappy over this single room which would serve as our bath, dining and bedroom?

My parents' passive attitude confirmed my fears, as the first the hours turned into days, weeks, months and years, yet no reason or explanations were given for relocating to this little shack. Those first few days were a blur once the dust had settled, and I was saddened I might never see my old friends again. We were to start a new life in this city, with the two single beds, a foam mattress, one brown single wardrobe, and two wooden tables—one as a kitchen work surface, the other for storage and packing. Someone donated an old kitchen cupboard while the only chair stood near the door, and a small mirror hung on the wall above it. A medium-sized round plastic basin to be used for bathing stood below the chair. Once all the clothing, footwear, crockery and cutlery were packed away, we had a tiny space, shaped like a T, in which to move about. If someone had told me the next nine years were going to be spent in this tiny shack, I might have offered to walk back to Wentworth.

Yes, so for the said nine years, we ate, slept and bathed in the same room. We washed or basically topped and tailed while the other family members were asleep or dashed behind the shacks or used the outside toilet. Other shack dwellers fought for space too, as well as for some semblance of privacy. One kettle full of boiled water did the trick and with everyone asleep, it was a semi-nude run back and forth. The toilet attached to the main house was used by everyone, and one had to make sure there was paper at hand. Not necessarily a roll of toilet paper, as I previously explained. Multiple flushing for those pesky floaters, and extended use of electricity whilst in the toilet was not tolerated, so sitting in the dark became a habit. Of course, the constant knocking hampered ablution duties as well. The area behind the shacks came in handy when waiting was not an option. I shall say nothing further.

Everyone slept at the same time. My father's coughing and snoring spells kept us awake most of the night. Interrupted sleeping patterns were the norm and after I wrote the book, I realized the origin of my disturbed sleeping cycles. Curled up at my dad's feet on a single bed, I was doomed. The flimsy curtains were no good either, and thin wooden walls ensured we heard every single sound. I would never wish those next nine years on anyone, dear or queer. Everyone welcomed us to East London until we became part of the furniture, yet I felt like the new kid on the block, if not displaced.

The first few days and weeks in the shack are a complete blank. We settled down to life as we knew it. Did I imagine a coat of despair shrugged over my parents at night? Neither voiced their feelings, but I noticed that my parents, especially my mother, were not happy about the new home. I might have prayed that it was one bad dream. Regardless of the shack and cramped quarters, there was a big city and neighbourhood to explore and new friends waiting in the wings. Most importantly, a brand-new school awaited my siblings and me.

Resigned to the life of a shack dweller, not exactly from riches to rags, we rallied and settled, and earlier strangers became friends. Everyone scraped to make ends meet and made the most of bad situations. The previous three years following Harvey and his game, the rest of the boys and bullies, were merely a foretaste of what lay ahead. My cousin and friends moulded me into a docile and passive miniature gay boy, who told no one he was emotionally tough, though ill-prepared for what was to follow.

Over the years I told friends or explained incidents, editing details to suit the person or listener. It became easier when you added a comical story in the mix to downplay the pain and hurt I felt at the time, disregarding the aftermath of emotions and deep sense of shame. Some might know, understand or even recall the next few chapters as I dug deep to express and expose feelings I had to keep hidden for so long. Those nicely edited stories I skimmed over or satirized, prevented probing questions, sympathy and disbelief. It was the easy way out since I felt ashamed, angry and annoyed that we moved.

I made a big effort to keep my home situation a secret and wanted everyone to think I lived in a real house with an inside toilet and bathroom. Nobody had to know I shared the same room with my parents and siblings. Facing away from my father's feet, I had the joys of many restless nights, staring at the wallpaper in the semi-darkness. Living in such close quarters, our personal, emotional, and physical isolation might be hard to understand. There was certainly no brotherly love or affection. His actions spoke a million words, yet no one mentioned the fact, but I did my best to please him, yearning for approval at every turn.

Perhaps I blocked or displaced certain events I had no control over, scared to expose painful memories and protecting myself from future emotional or psychological pain. Dreadful experiences overshadowed some wonderful encounters, denting my social if not daily life. No one was prepared to accept my identity, ruining much of my future happiness and potential in a society bent on scarring me for life. Alone and insecure, I struggled along, quiet and emotionless, burying all the misery in the hope it would be forgotten and excused. If only it was that simple.

From the age of nine to seventeen, I was this sad, isolated and lonely boy, not always by choice, ignorant of the psychological damage until it was far too late. To the few I call friends and acquaintances, my life has gone full circle, though some might disagree. But to all the readers and new friends I have made during editing, welcome to my world, a past and present tale.

My family had moved from a large shack to a real house and back to another shack in a matter of three years, leaving me shocked and confused. Our new home was assembled in Bond Street, found in the coloured township of CC Lloyd. Depending on the accents, all the locals called it Dukash or Dookarsh, and there was nothing dashing or debonair about the street or place.

Chapter 17: shocked and shunted into a brand-new school

Unknown relatives and neighbours helped us settle in, and soon the early commotion of the barracks became a distant memory as new sounds, different voices and accents greeted our sleepy senses. Word spread of our arrival, people openly spoke about us, assuming our understanding of Afrikaans was stunted. People translated or explained as we listened with wry amusement. Coloureds from Durban were known for having limited conversational skills when it came to Afrikaans, our second language. For the genuinely interested and intrigued, strangers popped in to stare, greet or enquire as to who we were and why we were in the area.

Our new yard was big. Despite the main house and shacks, there was ample space for a car or two. A small cemented walkway led to the door of the main house, and there was some semblance of a garden, populated by weeds and flowers. A hydrangea tree cask a huge shadow near the gate. Wire fencing surrounded the yard and larger gate for a car. Hard sand covered the whole yard area, and mismatched slates of fencing, planks and barbed wire separated us from our neighbours. Bolts, chains or padlocks kept the uninvited outside. Ropes, wires or twine strung along fencing or poles supported our drying laundry as we argued over space and rearranged washing accordingly. Behind our row of shacks was an overgrown area used as a shortcut, but yard owners were not always happy with trespassers taking liberties, nor were the bored or hungry dogs.

Of course, there were different rituals and activities around the place, and adjusting would take some time. In the barracks, we had practically lived on top of one another, with some margins for privacy. Now we had virtually none. There was no easy camaraderie, but it was early days yet, so everyone treated us like the people we were, outsiders. Most of them were friendly, yet wary, so we watched, getting to know some of the trespassers and characters around the place. Noise levels and partying histrionics were virginal in relation to our past experiences. Free from drug-fueled fights and police raids, we sat back and hoped to work with everything made available to us.

Our bathing option less ideal. We fought for use of the toilet every morning. The basic cistern with its rusty chain in the outside toilet was an added sore point. Usually busy and in demand, it was no fun braving cold and wet weather again, pulverized paper in hand. A blocked toilet and raw bottoms became the norm, and when nature called in a hurry, a dash behind the shacks was the next best option. Loitering dogs watched one suspiciously. Sometimes it was a long wait for the next caller if no paper was at hand, and a voice reminded users about water wastage when trying to flush floaters away.

The single tap near the toilet was our only source for running water, which we kept in containers inside the shack. Water was heated on the portable paraffin Primus stove, a slow process during cold winter months, which were much harsher in East London, as we would soon find out. The summer months made bathing in the small round basin a bit easier, or a quick splash under the tap did the trick. Face and underarms sorted, we used the toilet to clean up privately. Despite the inconveniences, cleanliness was next to Godliness in our shack. Before we could afford decent toothbrushes, fingers or bits of rag were used to scrub and clean our mouths. I cannot recall using a toothbrush for the first time.

Adjusting to our tiny shack took time. I felt uncomfortable as months turned into a year and more followed, with no signs of us being sent to live in a proper house. Our single beds and headboards remained second-hand, as did the replacement bedding or other household goods donated by friends and relatives. Those framed scriptures and pictures or quotes for a safe or happy home seemed out of place. Faded photos and an eternal rotation of embroidery and flowery patterned wall paper completed the look from the inside of our shack. Our mirror fell so many times, we stopped caring about those seven years of bad luck. Ragged bits of mirrored glass were taken along for a top and tail session. My mother made sure our shack was always neat and tidy.

Throughout my life, everything spelled a sense of déjà vu, because I felt everything was merely a repeated episode, me the constant character. As before, weather conditions played the worst jokes on shack dwellers. Water dripped through gaps, hailstones, heavy rains or strong winds rattled and bashed the flimsy building materials. The wet and damp kept us shivering for days, exacerbating my mother's asthma and her husband's coughing. I watched them suffer in silence, both weathering the storms each year, as we all hoped things would be different the next time around. The hot summer weather offered little respite as everyone complained, yet nothing changed, we merely fixed and adjusted. Shack dwellers came and went, yet the Calverley family remained in one place. Nine years of pure torture followed. Well that was how I viewed it. You may wonder why I was being so melodramatic about my situation when it was virtually the norm around the township?

Despite our living conditions, I remained emotionally isolated and separated from my family. Mentally battered and scarred after Harvey and the subsequent bullying, I had distanced myself from those closest to me, afraid they would react and treat me like it was my fault for being a sissy. My brother ignored me, and perhaps new relatives might do the same. What about my parents and sister?

I think people may have realized my physical, mental and emotional responses were a bit different in comparison to boys my age. Feeling like an impostor in my own home, while kids treated me almost as a leper on the playground, was hard and harsh. Things were going to get even tougher around my new neighbourhood. The ensuing chapters will take you through the next nine years of my daily life. While everyone scrimped to make ends meet, I did my best to fit in, please everyone, and feel accepted for who and what I was. I faced the battles, physical and mental, on my own, showing little or no emotion. Friends and strangers bombarded me with ideas, opinions and judgement on how to walk, talk or behave. No one was going to allow me to be myself and I was hell-bent on fighting them all the way.

Our move provided me with a fresh start, since no one knew my pedigree and I could hide the inner turmoil, but my actions, behaviour and responses outed me, so to speak. The small living space drove me into a self-imposed mental isolation, afraid my inner thoughts and feelings would be exposed to those who never spoke about them. Their silence drove me to hide and suppress my playground persona. As I grew older, it was unfortunate that my family and I became virtual strangers, filling me with an awkward sense of social awareness and interaction, carving a deep timidity and insecurity into someone hiding a shy yet exuberant playground personality.

Sharing a shack with thin walls made things difficult at times, and my mother saw no reason why we had to catch up on sleep during the day. What if visitors came calling? Only sick or lazy people slept during the day, she preached, a constant flow of noise, music and human traffic in the yard making any rest period near impossible. We had a lot to learn about our new neighbours and when the sun set, no one knew what went on behind the bolted shack door. I told no one I slept at the foot end of a single bed, a frozen adolescent, avoiding any physical contact with his father sleeping a few inches away.

What began as an innocent friendship around the shacks started a chain of events that set the tone for the next few years, and perhaps my adult life. I bore the heartache and misery, loneliness and fought down tears. Bottling my inner anguish, I opted to show a brave face to the outside world while they dented my individuality along the gravel dusty roads and very public corners.

Following a group of noisy kids as many gawked and pointed, we snaked along dusty roads, using shortcuts and paths to reach my new allocated school. Praying I would not give any sign of being a sissy, I bounded along in my white shirt and short grey school pants. My natural reaction to stares and whispers kicked into overdrive, a blank facial expression falling into place, my adopted coping mechanism. After detouring into the school office, someone escorted me to my classroom. I heard my name being called a few times as I was introduced as the new kid in town. Everything blurred as I joined a noisy group of thirty-two classmates. My siblings and I were new pupils at Pefferville Primary School. "Knowledge is Power" was the adopted motto. Read and enjoy, I say to you!

Chapter 18: pefferville primary school, an accent apart

My new school was a short walk from the shack, involving a similar route as my first one. That sense of having done this before surfaced as kids plodded along uneven dirt lined roads, pavements and well-trodden pathways, creating new shortcuts as the irate owners sent their barking dogs after us. My similar trips to Collingwood School came to mind until they faded into a memory bank. Stragglers scaled fences to avoid a curt public reprimand or punishment, the wire fencing dismantled in places after several, if not many, desperate pupils and pedestrians used the school grounds as a shortcut. We all knew tardiness was a grave offence.

A single road led in and out of the only gate, cars lined the tarmac near the office, and a small garden displayed flowers and shrubs, while short trimmed hedges were dotted along the cemented corridors. Small trees were scattered around a grassy area used as a school play and sports ground at the back, as well as three square areas of tarmac to be our assembly point and sporting grounds. Dense bushes and trees straddled a fence needing repairs. A huge open field lay beyond the fence and sounds from the Douglas Smith Highway filtered through windows and thin prefabricated walls. Loud screams of obscenity from passing pedestrians had us in stitches, their verbal acoustics giving some light relief, often disturbing classes. A few feet from the school gates stood the Kadalie Hall, used by the school and community.

The hall was named after Clements Kadalie, a teacher from Malawi. He moved to our country in the early 1900's and founded the Industrial and Commercial Workers' Union of Africa, opposing unfair labour laws while asking for decent workers' rights. Racial animosity was about to rear its ugly head in South Africa at the time, and Mr Kadalie fought huge battles against the ruling white South African regime. He settled in the coastal city of East London, now my new hometown, becoming the provincial organizer of the ANC or African National Congress—the present-day ruling government—and sadly he died in 1951.

With no idea how much the above history lesson would affect my own school, social, and adult life, I looked forward to each day at my new school. I was informed that I had to join my new classmates and write the impending June examination. Despite a different set of class lectures, they wanted to assess our level of education and progress. Nervous about messing up, I focused on the kindest, most beautiful teacher I had ever seen.

Mrs. Conway was tall and slim with thick glossy black hair, a lovely smile, and never raised her voice. She exuded a quiet poise and authority in the classroom, expecting diligent and respectful pupils in return. Wanting to do well, be good, get praised and please her as the new student was all that mattered. What a positive change from the last ogre in Durban who caned us over the slightest mistake. Far from being a troublemaker, there was nothing to fear because I had been nurtured to be docile. My introduction into the class and school system, though vague, had gone smoothly and I had no idea the next four years would be something of a challenge for the boy who sounded very different from the rest of his classmates.

They teased and imitated me playfully at every turn, shy and self-conscious, yet I felt no malice in their actions. I joined in the fun at my expense and with no idea about my past, I felt like a whole new person on the surface. 'Teacher,

Teacher, Teacher,' they shouted towards the front of the class, while I addressed her as 'Miss' as they listened to me speak, spell or read, the spell broken by someone laughing at my enunciation of certain words. It was clear I joined a crazy bunch of kids, with pleasant, nice teachers, and though I hated being the centre of attention, there was no escape from this happy crew of mixed learners and educators.

On one side, my sister Rosie was, for some reason, a year behind Frank, her younger brother. They were in standards 4 and 5, respectively, so it was clear Frank was a very clever child and my sister and I were the slower pair. Rumoured to have spent some time in the Transkei as a child, was it possible she missed a few years of school? They also said she had been fluent in the local black languages, yet there was not a trace of it in her speech. Using the examination as an excuse, I kept a low profile around the shack and school. The inquisitive stares, giggling or questions eventually petered out, and no one made much fuss over my physical presence, except when I opened my mouth.

We fretted over books and studied, or at least I did, and once everything was over, we would race away to enjoy our school holidays. Other than the history exam paper, no one knew much of Dick King in East London, and everything went fine. There was much more to learn about my new city later, if I made the grade. Awaiting report cards, we tidied up the classrooms for our return after the school holidays. On the final day, we were given our report cards alphabetically, eager to see how our marks, but warned it was the parents' duty to open the sealed envelope. Naturally we ripped them open and kids raced home with excitement, others dragged feet home in despair. I was proud to see I had made the grade, if only just. A passing grade was all I wanted, though the shame of coming twenty-eighth hurt somewhat. All was not lost as we had another examination to show what we were made of. Rosie fared no better than I, while Frank proved that he was as bright as expected.

On the lighter side, my pretty sister was chosen as the new Carnival Queen, despite it being a misjudgment over the school favourite. How dare an outsider win the sash and plastic crown? My sister was friendly, sweet and lovely, and she deserved to win. I was so proud of her, and it put us in the spotlight. Fame by association, and after the carnival, we tried to find our own little niche in the classroom, around the playground and in the community.

Scouting for friends was no hard task, yet I held back, trying to identify where I fit in. Should I befriend the girls, connect with the boys or avoid them, be myself until it all came crashing down around me? A mental wreck, I fought down painful memories of being teased and taunted. My interaction with girls and boys was measured, hiding a secret and fighting down feelings I had little or no control over. Hesitant to join in the games and play, I politely refused invitations, past experiences clouding an eagerness to be accepted as a friend or part of a team. I was not boisterous and abrasive, and soccer and football, cricket and rugby, were never going to be part of my repertoire in life. If these unrestrained boys kept their hands and lips off me, my secret would not be uncovered, I lied to myself. My thoughts were hardly cold when I met another boy I happened to call a friend. Unfortunately, we were beacons for the bullies and tyrants on very different levels.

Chapter 19: a bullied twosome and a sprint in time

It was only a natural for two outsiders to meet and be friends. We sat a few feet apart in class yet gradually found ourselves spending time around each other during breaks. He dark-skinned and slightly built, with short wavy black hair and eyes. He exuded an aura of someone suffering from an illness. They said he had a hole in his heart, a kid prone to fits and fainting spells. We all understood little about his condition and he never spoke about it, but the other kids belittled and taunted him because of it. Exempt from any sport or vigorous activities, his lips, nails and skin were a dark and dusky colour. Always short of breath, Irwin wore clothes suited for winter weather throughout the year. A high-necked collar, or polo neck, a thick checked or plaid shirt worn over or under his school uniform, was his trademark outfit. His attire, physical attributes, and symptoms attracted the bullies, but he was too feeble and weak to fight back.

After being verbally abused and bullied for over two years, it was strange watching it happen to someone else. Irwin had no control over his illness and he could not run or escape the baying crowds. They followed us to his house, shouting, teasing, goading him for a response. Laughing at his weak attempts at courage, Irwin gasped for air as his tormentors remained merciless, intent on being top class verbal aggressors. I was ignored and shoved aside in the commotion, too scared to intervene and face them. It was not cool being the freaky kid in school. I was merely the odd one out and not yet guilty by association.

His fingertips were rounded and thick, the nails curved, so the baying bullies begged to see his witch nails or claws, only to flee in mock horror and glee when he obliged. Many years later I learned that clubbed fingers, dyspnoea or shortness of breath, and a bluish discolouration of the skin, or cyanosis, were signs of cardiopulmonary disease. Born that way, my friend suffered for his illness while I had a different anomaly, not something I gained from birth. I had chosen to be this way or made to behave and act like a girl. Irwin was not like me, yet we both suffered at the hands of bullies. We all felt sorry for him, sometimes others stood up for him while I watched passively from the side-lines, except when things got out of hand.

Bullies were not the only ones who took advantage of Irwin's symptoms. Feigning his fainting spells, which caused chaos and disruption in or out of class, we often called a bluff to avoid an impromptu test or examination. Someone had to dash for the smelling salts while we secretly rejoiced, hoping he was acting up. It was bad and wrong, but I knew it was a way to feel part of the class even though no one called him a friend. On his way home, he often had a real fit, and everyone fled while I remained until he was out of it. Concerned adults rushed to his aid but sometimes he did it to stop the taunts. Warned beforehand, it was painful to see him suffer when he did not feign an epileptic fit. After a few weeks and months, they got bored or felt he had suffered enough and focused their attention onto his sissy friend, me.

Leaving Irwin outside his home, I walked to my own shack, heckled by the kids for nothing more than being his friend. I cannot recall if he ever invited me in or if I said no, and I was never going to ask him to come around to my tiny shack. My secret was yet undiscovered since we never spoke about the bullies from my past. However, that was about to change.

The good-natured teasing in class continued, my pronunciation the ice breaker. They tittered, and I laughed as I recited the poem I knew and loved at the time, Grasshopper Green by Nancy Dingham Watson. Recited for fun, amid squeals of laughter, I gladly entertained them about a cheerful grasshopper who lived under a hedge so gay. How very apt, except my cheerful character was contrived. Outside the classroom, it was I who became the spectator, until the tide turned against me.

With very little memory of my first two schooling years, the ensuing ones are painted into my brain cells. There were so many issues among the pupils, somewhat frivolous, competitive, but both entertaining. We had separate English and Afrikaans pupils, and the animosity was palpable around the place. Each thought they were better and more deserving than the other, feuds breaking out over sporting events, examinations or the games during break times. It was 'us' against 'them' as we judged each other on looks, social standing and grey cells, jeering accordingly. No one seemed to care that we were in a similar boat, poverty-stricken and fighting to make ends meet. The prettier were the adored angels, straight locks and hair threads were envied and colourful irises were to be resented. Ridiculed for the lack of the physical traits, the rest of us watched, somewhat jealous or sympathetic. Poor but pretty was good they said, the less attractive were disregarded as lesser mortals, irrespective of personality or talent and brains. No one gave any thought how nasty we were to one another at the time.

My turn to be in the spotlight began in an awkward fashion. We always played at the edge of the school grounds, using cardboard and taking turns to slide down the grassy slopes. Pulling and pushing each other, no one saw the pile of dog shit until it was too late. Since I was the pusher, I got blamed and all eyes turned on me. I kept a very low profile for a while. Sadly, the poor unfortunate classmate had a fatal accident at home, dying at a very young age. May her soul rest in peace.

My twenty-eighth place in my initial examinations became a distant memory. I had to impress my teachers, so I worked hard, my grades improved, and I got singled out. The compliments made me more self-conscious and uncomfortable. Suppressing my joy so others could take centre stage, Irwin and I stayed close friends, the bullies lingering a few feet away. Physical education and training took place on black squares of tarmac and huge expanse of grass behind the school. Netball, hockey, soccer, cricket, rugby, athletics and exercises, like present-day boot camp, depended on the weather or equipment and enthusiasm of pupils and teachers. We bickered over tarmac space and tossed a coin, the losing tutor and pupils sulked, sometimes disrupting games or gym classes. Heavy rains, hot humid days and strong winds kept us inside, a free period to run amok or catch up with homework.

During one of these sporting sessions, we got to race each other as teachers searched for candidates to join teams for sports day, usually athletics. I was fast enough to join the blue team, competing against the red, green, yellow and orange teams. Two boys in my class, Nathan and Jeremy, became my rivals on the running field and later, track—well, not the kind of athletics tracks we have now. Kids supported a team instead of a classmate as we joined in the singing, dancing and cheering, for friends and enemies alike. Roles were reversed to gain maximum points, forgiving past slights on the day. If one had no hoarse voice or sore throat the next day, one clearly did not have a good outing at all. Carrying that croaking voice with pride and honour, the winning athletes were admired as much as their supporters with cracked and gruff voices. Enjoying the excitement, I had no idea I was being watched and monitored. In all the excitement, I let my guard down and he made the first move.

I would spend about four and half years at Pefferville Primary School and it was such a whirlwind of activity as we ran around being kids. Unsure when it all changed for a shy insecure little boy, the time had come and there was no turning back. There was a weak spot, exposing a quiet determination and anguish to conceal my past after doing my utmost to hide the loneliness I felt during and after school. Although I saw Irwin as a friend, I really had no one to talk to about who and what I really had become. My cousin and the boys had shaped me into the adult I am today, alone, shy and insecure, yet no one ever sees that side of me. The word damaged may be a harsh term, but for now it will do. Instead, I gave them the extroverted, confident and bubbly version of myself, a theatrical facade I cultivated to overcome a fear of being in the public eye.

You are very welcome to wear my polished black Bata Toughees, and we shall retrace my steps on the dusty roads, meander along well-trodden and dirt-lined pathways. Toughees, the shoes, were specifically designed for school kids in South Africa, who walked long distances, to and from school. They were also good for running, jumping and durable for any ball sports, not to mention a well-aimed kick to the shin area in some cases. Luckily, or perhaps not, I was spared physical pain, which might have been better than the emotional agony I had to face. All I did was fight back tears, ignoring the spiteful verbal jabs from strangers, playmates and peers. Do hold on tight.

Chapter 20: enduring adolescence, the most painful of pleasures

Then it happened. Along my daily route to school, lived eleven-year-old Shawn, dark skinned, curly haired, with a perfect set of white teeth. An only child. Shawn was a boisterous and confident boy about two years older than I. We thought he was very spoilt, yet he became what we now call a friend with benefits. They lived in a proper house and my friend enjoyed a luxurious soak in a huge white bath tub every night, a luxury I could not afford, before bedtime. Dream and hope was all I did.

Shack dwellers were treated like second-class citizens by some people, and the kids were no different. Shawn attended an Afrikaans-speaking school and requested a bit of help with his English homework. I offered, spending more and more time in his home, often prolonging my visits unnecessarily. Surrounded by electricity, some real home comforts in his own small room, I envied the idea as my whole family lived in a shack of similar size. I took my job seriously, helping him enunciate, read and write better English.

Early one evening, I trekked over, was informed he was bathing, and insisted I wait. It was no fun hearing him splash about, my last bath a mere memory, even though it was much smaller than the one they owned. I was not sure if he planned his bathing time to our lessons, but it happened a few times before he asked me to join him in the bathroom. I refused, his mother supporting my decision, asking him to get done and not waste the water. Often kids bathed first, and parents used the same water.

155

Shawn sat in a huge white ceramic bath filled with steaming water as bubbles floated around his dark shoulders, the dim light glinting off his shiny skin. As I perched on a rickety wooden stool, we chatted while I fought the urge to jump into the bath. It was never going to happen, and neither was any offer going to be extended.

After months of topping and tailing from a round plastic basin, he never saw the envy in my eyes, thanks to the red globe and steam. We were welcome to use the fridge for storage, cook on their electric stoves in an emergency, but the ceramic bath was not a communal accessory. I did not understand the specifics about hygiene at the time, and not all things were to be shared with strangers. Limits and boundaries existed in other homes, or those made of bricks and cement. Our nightly bathroom charades cemented our friendship, it being the first time I visited another kid's home consistently. No one mentioned the term close friends yet, as I watched him soak among the bubbles, very dark and happy as his doting servant kept him company, awaiting the next directive.

I told no one about the night time ritual and felt less self-conscious around my naked friend. Aware of my past and what was done to me, I refused when he asked me to be helpful and scrub his back. A typical boy with no inhibition, he stood up and turned a gleaming wet back for me to wash. I timidly carried out the task, afraid to touch him. Thus, started a game of touch and tease. Picking up on my shyness, he splashed water over me and while scrubbing his back, attempted to get me into the bath. I resisted, a bit too meekly, internally crying over the injustice. Shawn was playing a game while I genuinely wanted to hop in beside him. Our simulated fights alerted his mother, he was told to stop messing about, leave me alone and get out of the bathroom. I wanted it to go on forever, I moaned to myself.

Bathroom fights and homework times were a drawn-out affair, which meant I got to overstay my welcome until dinner time. Either I was offered leftover morsels on a plate or I quietly retreated through the back door before dinner was served. I judged the time and tried to play my cards right, assessing the mood as time passed. Poor kids knew all the signals when it came to sharing food, snacks or goodies. One was either left alone in the room, your friend called out to eat out of sight in the kitchen, the smell of food and spoons scraping on enamel plates echoing the growling in your belly. On the rare occasion, Shawn entered the room with an extra plate, the smaller portion given to me. We studied and ate, and I thought of my siblings who went to sleep after a cup of tea and slices of bread covered in jam, syrup or peanut butter. This extra meal was heavenly, yet I went home to eat the meagre sandwich, hiding the fact I had had a good cooked meal somewhere else.

My time with Shawn was my secret, and I told no one how much I liked being around him. I saw him as my bigger boyfriend, and the idea made me feel all girly and loved, even though he had no idea about how I felt. He directed the time we spent doing our homework, which was less since we played games and he teased me relentlessly. The body scrub evolved into rubbing a layer of cocoa butter or Vaseline on his back. Shawn waved his boy thing at me, telling me he got it cut or circumcised in hospital. I was a bit clueless, but his did look different to my own and I had no intention of showing it at all. Averting my eyes, he waved it in my direction whenever he felt the need. I had to maintain my composure, but it was clear that I was different on so many levels. We all laughed when his mother caught him waving his willy at me.

When I didn't appear, he sought me out, even if to apply the lotion and nothing else. I thought of Harvey and his initiation during an innocent game of hide and seek. Is this another one of those? Shawn insisted I apply the lotion on his entire body, grabbing my hands when I stopped short of his private areas. We jostled and wrestled, assured he had no idea of my past. This time, however, we were playing a game on my terms, despite my acting up like a tempestuous maiden.

Had he done this before or with another boy? Shawn enquired about my shyness and awkwardness around other boys. Of course, he knew the answer, and before I gave an answer, he pounced, wrestling me down onto the single bed. I had lost the bet and we spent even less time doing homework, his play fighting taking centre stage. His main aim was to pin me to the bed and win, but I was no weakling by any standards. Letting him overpower me, I squirmed clumsily, staring up at him. Assured a friendship built on homework was about to change, I struggled and shook my head at the realization it was no longer a game.

Ordering me to stop, I refused, bucking and trying to push him off, as his face moved closer. I was forced to keep my head still and he placed his lips onto mine, waiting to see how I would react. Holding my breath, I gave little resistance, realizing my friend had done this before. Whether it had been with another boy or girl, I would never ask, and surrendered to his darker lips as he kissed me. It felt so right and after this, I vowed not to fight back. Well, not that vigorously anyway.

For the first few days and weeks, the air between us felt different and charged. Shawn bathed, I dried and applied the lotion to his back. All this was done as a preliminary exercise for the main event, our wrestling match and what was to follow. I played the part of a girl to perfection, affronted by his forwardness and assumption I should succumb to him. I had the emotional and mental strength, he the physical, yet we both shared some experience. It was vital I play the part of a girl, or the illusion would be shattered, and I did not want that to happen.

Our child-like kisses were chaste as we giggled and pretended to fight when his mum checked on us over the sudden prolonged silences. We hardly spoke much, taking the short breaks for air before he held me down again.

Naturally, this would be our secret and I walked around happy that I had a secret boyfriend, who was very different from Harvey or Clinton. This time I wanted him to wrestle and kiss me. Dragging my body back to the shack, I curled up near my father's feet on the single bed, my face red hot, lips tingling from a pleasure I could not fully understand. I relived it all as I fell into a deep sleep, unaware the feelings I felt were nothing to be ashamed of, by any means.

Shawn's room housed two single beds, and sometimes I could sleep over. Being able to stretch in my own sleeping space was great. Mind you, I did spend most of the night curled up next to him, but that was different. We waited long enough his mother to settle before I was dragged under the covers, kissed and held until he slept.

His mother often found us in the morning, curled up next to each other and never said a word since we were both boys, innocent and chaste. While Shawn honed his kissing and cuddling skills on his pliant friend, we both knew our secret game would come to an end. He was certainly not like me. Mixing with the other kids was a bit tricky as we tried to hide the closeness we shared behind a closed door. I allowed him to make decisions, fawned over him like a love-struck teenager. It was obvious I had no idea how to behave around boys, nor act like one. Comfortable in the knowledge that Shaun knew the real me and had my back, I veered towards the girls, seeking the emotional fulfilment and acceptance I so deeply craved. Slowly but surely, everyone adopted the idea I was no ordinary boy, and not a real girl either, but I told nobody I belonged to Shawn after dark. We were boyfriend and girlfriend.

The said boyfriend wanted to mark my neck with a hickey or love bite, but I was not to be publicly branded or seen as a willing participant, not that anyone knew about what we were doing. He kept begging, so I let him leave a red mark under my chin. During a game, it was noticed, and everyone teased me about it, asking who had left it. I was to open a door and path carved by Harvey and the rest before Shawn, unaware of the sad and painful future bearing down on me. If I had known, I might have milked every piece of joy I shared with my gentle dark-skinned friend.

Chapter 21: childish pranks, pleasures and pain

After school, I only had eyes or lips for Shawn. I had to hide my joy, but it felt good if not emotionally satisfying. I wanted to please him, yet when he stuck his tongue into my mouth, I jerked my head away in shock, but my boyfriend was insistent I learn the art of French kissing. It took a few seconds to convince me and he showed me how it was done. Shawn made it feel so natural, despite the fact we had to kiss or cuddle out of sight. Alone or surrounded by my own family, I felt like a fraud. Feeling happy and comfortable, I could not shake off the inner guilt and shame. We could stay out till way after sundown in the seventies, so I made full use of the chance to hide with Shawn or be alone to think about everything happening around me.

The dusty little road in front of the shack overlooked a huge forest, which we called a bush. There were houses dotting the horizon, and it would take a few years before I set foot in that area. Informed that richer people lived there, I had no reason to doubt and question. Out of reach and out of touch, I focused on my space and the piles of rubbish left a few feet away. A small ditch off the road was used as a dumping site. Rotting food or waste and broken goods became a haven for scavenging cats, dogs, rats, flies, insects and vagrants.

During games, arguments ensued among kids designated to collect balls, bats or toys from the stinking rubble while we pushed each other over the edge as we swore and scrambled away in disgust and anger. We ignored warnings to keep clear since it was such a fun game, parents not overly fussed that we hopped around piles of rat-infested junk—just do not come home crying or hurt. A health hazard or not, heavy rain or heat waves made the situation worse. Dead rats, or cats and dogs killed by passing cars, got flung into the pile of debris, ensuring Bond Street was a buzzing zone of flies, mosquitoes and insects, intent on keeping us awake at night. I have lived to tell this tale, so it is a miracle my friends and I were not stricken with any horrible infections at the time.

All the above antics and issues never hindered forays into the dense forest, for fun or a dare. People created gardens to grow some fruit and vegetables. Strawberry plots were the sweetest temptation. There were many fruit trees dotted around the place, yet we still plundered and poached. At the bottom of the forest ran a tiny shallow creek, teeming with frogs, crabs, and tadpoles. We chased butterflies, grasshoppers, shot at the birds using a homemade catapult while others pelted them with stones. We played a game of dolly house, still very much innocent from the kind I had played before. Stolen and plundered goods, be it animal or vegetable, were cleaned and cooked over a fire. Kids were defensive about specific territories in the forest, often clashing over space. Fight or flee, as stones were thrown when one was outnumbered, or a fist fight was impossible.

A group of boys and girls joined forces, and we enjoyed the fruits of the forest. Daddy and sons built a makeshift home and hunted for food while the girls cleaned and got a meal ready. The leader designated roles and everyone played out family life under the bright sun while birds, grasshoppers, bees, butterflies and croaking frogs added sound and colour. Sound of traffic and distant voices carried in the wind and while roles and jobs were changed during every dolly house game, nobody bothered that I could stay home with the girls, not joining the boys in hunting for food. If I did, my job was to be a watchdog and not much else, yet I was more than capable of climbing a tree or scaling a fence. I was more than happy to be the sister, never the brother, father or mother. It was a joke, on me naturally, and a short-lived one at that. When no girls were around, I stood in and took over the role, with relish I might add! No one knew about all those other duties I performed as mother of the house in the barracks, and no one knew how close I was to Shawn, often the daddy in the game.

After the meals, games were played, the boys wrestling in the long grass, scaring one another with insects and grasshoppers. We chased butterflies, racing after hares and a rat or two. Sometimes we braved the wet weather, the overflowing creek providing the extra diversion at times. Shawn and I acted out a wrestling tussle, a prelude for me to run and hide. He would follow, find me and hold me while I playfully fought him off until he kissed me into submission, out of sight. We always returned alone, unaware a flushed face, neck and my stinging lips were giving the game away. Tired and happy, we rested on flattened cardboard boxes, cramped beds, spaces, and shacks forgotten. It felt like heaven on earth, bathed in a childish innocence, yet I felt very isolated from it all.

Our friends were not as stupid or slow as we thought, and I got teased when given the role of the sister or mother. It was obvious what was going on between Shawn and me, but no one mentioned it out loud. In his absence, another boy took me aside and I gave no resistance. There were the usual attempts at play fighting until he pinned me down under him, a new set of lips caressing my own. Had Shawn told him or was he merely taking the opportunity to use me as many had in my past? It felt strange kissing someone other than Shawn, a situation I was going to get used to from this point and beyond.

Of all the games we played, an excursion into the forest was the finale. My role as the mother was cemented as boy after boy played the father. Everyone wanted a turn, the fact that I was a boy did not faze or bother them. I did not complain, nor stop or push them away but allow the constant stream of boys to use me as a kissing buddy. It was usually done out of sight and away from the others, yet everyone knew who had been before or after. At night, I belonged to Shawn, but during the day, I let any other boy walk me into the woods. All we did was wrestle and kiss, fully clothed, too afraid or a scared to go take that extra step as Harvey had done a year or two earlier. Naturally some looked at me as a freak, a boy being kissed by others and not putting up any fight. Initially it was a joke, and some felt sorry I was dragged away until it changed, and I found myself being taunted and teased. No one teased the boys kissing me. They were normal and blamed me for everything. Shawn, my boyfriend, kept a low profile when I was being bullied, yet tried to make up for it when I went to his room to study. Then he tried to make me feel better, yet never easing the emotional agony. Feeling his lips and arms around me was comforting. I felt appreciated, refusing to accept I was being used and fed to the bullies at the same time. Holding my head up high, I took it all on the chin and later my entire body.

The fun and games over, all niceties were pushed aside as things escalated quickly. It appeared every boy wanted to put his lips over my own. Small hands grabbed, pulled and held me down, while another hand roughly covered my mouth, stopping a scream for help. Nodding my head that I would not make a sound, fighting for air, they pinched and

164

bit my skin, biting, groping and kissing me. They were rough as they licked my neck, nipping at my skin, daring to leave a red bite mark. I begged them not to, my fear an added thrill. Some watched and never participated, yet no one raised a hand to rescue me. Once they were done, they dispersed and left me alone, bruised and hurting in the long grass. No one noticed the hurt in my eyes as they walked away, making fun of a sissy boy, getting what he deserved.

I had not turned thirteen yet and another sense of deja vu surfaced. Shawn and the brand-new posse of boys had cemented their presence into a routine I could not run or hide from. Of similar age or a bit older, they led me away or I was expected to follow submissively or run ahead, praying they would not be rough. A bunch of boys I knew dragged me into the bush amid cheers and teasing, my screams ignored, a game to many, with me being the brittle toy to be used and shunted aside later. Sore and bruised, I limped home, telling no one while hiding my shame and humiliation as much as I fought back the tears of frustration and helplessness. Did no one care how I felt?

Alternatively, I could not tell them how much I wanted and enjoyed what they did to me, perhaps encouraging them, but found their aggression too much to handle. I was a willing participant but was not allowed to touch or wrap my arms around them. My arms were held down, they used force while Shawn kissed me gently, erasing any bit of doubt about my true feelings. Bond Street was becoming too small as my fame and notoriety spread among the boys, and bullies, in the township.

I had flashbacks. After Shawn came Jeremy, Gabriel, Donald, Lester, Dennis, Patrick and Charlie, a regular bunch of kissing buddies. I was happy to circulate or be passed

165

around from one to the other. Whether some waited in line or dragged me away, there was a name for someone like me. Not all boys wanted to share their secret and I felt a bit wary around strange boys, expecting them to drag me away. The girls knew what I was up to, the marks under my chin proof and shown with pride. I tried hard to ignore the tittering around me, unsure if the adults heard about me, the weak lighting from a lamp and candle my saving grace in the small shack. Nothing could dampen my inner happiness when I rehashed the times I spent with my special boyfriend or many eager suitors, dismissing the angry boys waiting to use and bruise me.

Exposed or not, they all joked about what we were doing, except me of course. It was a game to them, but a reality for me. Privately pampered yet publicly persecuted, they played with my emotions, or I allowed them to dictate how I felt after they left me to gather my senses and dignity. The verbal goading and whispering gathered steam and resonated along the streets, paths and playground. Irwin, my sickly friend, had to see me face my tormentors this time around.

The bullying grapevine flourished among those seeking to impress or gain some brownie points among their peers. I watched Irwin suffer so I braced myself for what followed. I was slandered and mocked, named and shamed in front of new classmates and friends, my face turning bright red in embarrassment. Those taking my side were drowned out by the loud cursing. Calling me a moffie, slang for an effeminate man and male homosexual and holnaaier, a bum pusher. I wanted to cry and die of shame. Adding a bit more fuel, they wanted everyone to know I do rude like a dog.

166

They warned other kids I was filthy, and I might taint them with my horrible behaviour.

Their words cut deep and were extremely hurtful. Merely acting, thinking or playing like one of the girls, I hurt no one, yet I was labelled an outcast and harshly exposed. They were so cruel to Irwin and me, cementing layers of psychological pain and turmoil. For many of my years in primary school, I faced daily persecution for what I was and did. Some stories were false but correcting them was not going to change perceptions at all. Despite the public flogging, old and new suitors came calling, some eager to prove a point or a dare. I refused no one, aware they might physically restrain and hurt me.

Not every boy was happy to share me in a group, though he knew my other suitors. I had a secretive and shy admirer who wanted me alone and no one had to know about us. I wondered if he knew I had kissed his older brother. He was different, and I could see him wrestling with the idea of kissing another boy. There was this adolescent boy fighting internally, eyes darting around nervously, until curiosity and hormones made him decide. We played our own game of cat and mouse, seeking me out when he felt brave enough. I played the weaker role perfectly, afraid to scare this gentle boy away.

He never got over the fear of being found out and I never told anyone about him. Our favourite spot was behind a row of shacks, the roosting hens our only witnesses until they got spooked by something and he fled in sheer panic, assuming someone saw us kiss, ending our secretive liaisons.

In the slow twinkling of an eye, I lost count of the number of boys who chased, led or pulled me aside. From friend to suitor to tormentor, the only person remaining true or constant was the sissy boy, me. Powerless to refuse the boys, I secretly yearned to be wanted, loved and accepted as part of a group, to sell my soul, or lips, to the devil. What I needed was a very thick skin to survive and cope from one day to the other. Living a life bordering on the breadline and harassed by bullies, I tried to remain free-spirited and we made the most of what life offered under the circumstances.

Chapter 22: a boy for all seasons, with no rhyme or reason

The boys I kissed around the shack or in the forest often shunned me at school or on the playground. Others were daring and tried to isolate or drag me away while friends and kids chanted and laughed at my expense. Groups of boys circled and watched for an opportunity to grab and tease, my girlish reactions inciting them, while others saw me as a character to be used for entertainment. I was scared to leave the classroom for a toilet break or run an errand for a teacher. Disrupting a lesson was not appreciated, so being trapped in the toilet, I had no idea who pinched, grabbed or pulled at me as a pair of lips and teeth nipped at my face and neck. Hands clamped over my mouth and nose as I fought for air in panic.

Roaming prefects and teachers often looked the other way, assuming it was a game as boy after boy pounced, wrestled, pinched or grabbed at me. No one saw the kissing or fondling, but it was obvious what they were doing once I was dragged away and surrounded. Walking out to a score of animated kids, my face flushed, body parts and ego bruised, I never showed them how much I hurt inside. Unsure which affected me more, the public disregard or private debasement, my fear and panic increased when I had to go to toilet or venture out during school break or recess. Hiding out of reach only encouraged them to scream derogatory names in my direction, forcing a decision on my choice of punishment. Mortified, my self-consciousness doubled, watching my classmates witness my shame, the odd one trying to fight my corner. I felt more alone than ever.

While I endured physical and emotional bullying away from the classroom, my classmates took a playful swipe at my discomfort, grabbing out to me as I passed. Skittish and jumpy, I joined in the fun and games, affronted but secretly enjoying the attention. I chuckled at myself yet could not drown out the crude laughs echoing in my head. Irwin was the target for being medically ill, but my bullying stemmed from some unseen social flaw, manifesting in my unacceptable and displeasing affectations. I was healthy yet not the boy I was born to be. A sissy, there must be something wrong with me, they said, and I was not normal. For a very long time it seemed I was the only gay boy around, or the one most targeted. Other than Irwin, I cannot recall any other kids being demeaned as we were.

Everyone relished our public badgering, but I kept my pain a secret, finding it hard to cry in public, irrespective of the nature of their actions. Venturing into the forest on my own, I lay among the tall grass and only then did I allow the tears to fall. With no one to comfort me, feeling dejected and alone, I couldn't understand what drove boys to kiss me or why bullies disgraced and belittled me. I was doing nothing wrong and I had no idea what made me act the way I did. Watched by the birds and insects, I wept until my head hurt. Washing my face in the creek, I ignored prying eyes and mocking questions as I walked home and crept into bed. If anyone picked up on my sadness or swollen eyes, my family never asked any questions.

My public humiliation during school hours escalated even though I felt relatively safe while confined to the yard or classroom. The bullies only stopped when I became too stressed, or they got bored or were intimidated by a good

Samaritan. Beyond the school gates, I was on my own and at their mercy.

They waited for Irwin and me at the school gate, but nothing prepared me for the anger and attitudes I faced. The first time was a prelude as Irwin played second fiddle and I became the intended target as boys trailed and taunted us. He tried to scare them off, but they were adamant. Tackling me to the ground, everything became a blur as I felt rather than saw hands pulling at me, but I heard clapping, loud cheers and laughing as lips pressed onto my own. Someone else tried to bite my neck as I jerked and fought for air. I could not scream with the amount of bodies bustling over me and yet no one lifted a finger to save me. My dear friend had to witness it all. They walked away, too proud to care, a stone thrown at me for good measure. Straggling kids added insults, a few ignored me. Struggling to my feet, I dusted myself off and limped home in a daze and held my head high, defiant in my shame.

It became a habit for an army of boys to ambush me outside the school gates, begin a one-sided verbal ridiculing before pouncing. After a few scrums along the road, I fled into the nearby bush. Chased and flung onto the ground, among rotting leaves, debris and awful smells, I waited for them to finish and flee. Did I feel their anger for doing what they did, my acceptance adding to their disgust, justifying my punishment? The only medicine was to numb myself against the daily demoralization, finding solace or inner strength deep in the forest, secluded with my childish thoughts and reasoning. It felt better without an audience, I told myself, the falling tears soothing and calming a pain that would never be relieved.

No matter which way I turned, ran or walked, there would be someone or a group of kids heckling Irwin and me, or just me. Being left disheveled and emotionally battered along the dusty roads became a daily sight, but I refused to break down in public. Yet not all the boys around me were mean or bad. Andrew and I met in school, both loved to run and became rivals on the sports track. He played almost every other sport and was the typical boy I should have been. We bonded over our love of running and over time, I found myself drawn to this sporty dark-skinned boy and relished the time we spent on the playground. Rival or friend, he joined the other boys, good-naturedly teasing and provoking me, which I enjoyed and sometimes encouraged them. I was happy or even flirty one minute, only to have the rug pulled from under my feet as the bullies kicked me to the ground, not literally of course.

During the athletics season, Andrew and I gravitated towards one another, spending a lot more time together well after the sports day had ended. He loved cricket, soccer, volleyball and hockey, while I avoided or refused to join in. Stilted, bashful and averse to any form of aggression, I feared body contact most of all. Running was good for me; it alleviated my inner apprehension, turmoil and anxiety. Andrew joined me as a training partner, unsure who had initiated the partnership, but I had no issues with him by my side. I felt comfortable.

While Harvey had circled, cunning and predatory, Shawn innocently broke down my defenses, the other boys a mere formality. When Andrew came along, I was ready for whatever he threw at me. In fact, I wanted him to wrestle, grab and kiss me. Having a past riddled with unhappy experiences, my emotions were all over the place. Perhaps I had misread the signs and his friendship, expecting every boy who approached me to be interested in using me to hone their kissing skills.

Like those nightly baths, Andrew and I met to run, race and exercise until we ran out of steam or it was time to go home. At school, he joined the gang while I faded into a wallflower, ignored until our next training session. I had no hard feeling about that; it was the law of the playground. No one wanted to be seen with the sissy boy, in case it became a case of guilt by association. Yet alone on the running track, which was far from the school, and away from prying eyes, we were friends. When he suddenly sent me sprawling onto the grass, I was shocked, but he jumped, and we wrestled for some time before he pinned me under him. I strained in outrage, secretly rejoicing as I did a good impression of glaring back at him. Of course, we were on the same page after all this time, but I assumed and feared he would come to his senses and release me. A set of dark eyes stared back at me and I silently begged him to finish the task.

Shaking my head from side to side, I was not going to make it look that easy, the now familiar pattern engraved in my brain. He waited a few seconds, then dropped his face closer and closer. I struggled, but he held me firmly in place. Both silent, I watched in disbelief as his lips grew closer and opened my mouth to protest, but he had little and no intention of stopping. Our eyes locked before his lips touched my own and I could not believe he had done it. He sat astride me, held my hands above my head, I could not move and had no desire to do so, so I let my running buddy take control. I heard the cars race by along the nearby street, lost in the joy of kissing someone whom I really liked, and it felt good, natural and acceptable.

I have a recurring or rotating cycle of bad experiences, followed by a happy spell, fooling me into a false sense of elation and acceptance. Adored by one or two, only to be hated and ostracized by many. I took it on the chin, like the man I was not meant to become. Andrew and I kept our running track dalliances a secret, acting all distant in front of everyone around the school grounds. Soon, we did less racing or running, the wrestling and kissing taking up most of our time. It was difficult keeping quiet and not being able to share my joy with anyone, while the bullying had to be so very public and painful. I could not wait for the bell to toll, knowing I would meet up later and feel loved, even though he felt very different about what we were doing.

Every time he looked at me, I melted a little more. I let him kiss my mouth and neck, even as I made him fight me for it. Maintaining the illusion that it was a game coated the fact that I was another boy, my girlish screams adding to the fantasy in my head. One may say I had fallen in love, or something close to that, but what did I know about love as a primary school kid who lived in a shack? I was kissing a boy from the better side of town.

Concentrating in class felt like I was being punished, knowing he was some hundred feet away from me. Sometimes he stood up for me when the bullies came calling, and I liked him even more. I had Irwin as a friend and Andrew as my secret boyfriend, yet he never saw me as a girlfriend. I certainly lived with my little head in the clouds. We stayed kissing friends throughout primary school when, at the age of fourteen, he came to his senses and left me alone.

Kids treated me like an outcast, and I had no one to talk to or confide in. I had come to terms with the sissy tag and would never change. They let me know I was hateful and ugly, dirty and undeserving of friends. I flitted between games, standing in until a real boy or girl came along. Pushed towards the girls, and being treated like one, I found it easier to go along with the charade. I actively sought the connection, hoping it would appease the mental and emotional confusion heaped upon me. They expected feelings of shame whenever I made a public appearance. Any show of defiance was greeted by a storm of hatred and loathing.

I was bearing a cloak of misery, and few were sympathetic to my plight. I faced a daily dose of torment. I was silent and withdrawn as I ventured around the place, my calm exterior hiding myriad emotions. An urge to scream and shout or curse and blame Harvey for the path he created was overwhelming. Everyone called me a sissy and treated me like a girl, and yet my parents or siblings never mentioned or spoke about it. In the meantime, all I did was pander to the whims of those around me, trying to fit in, be a friend and not get into trouble.

One day after school, along with some other boys, I was invited to someone's house. Surprised, I tagged along, nervous yet excited to be included. Negotiating the grassy field and steep incline behind the school, we entered a very big house. The kitchen so much bigger than my shack. I had not set foot in such a posh house. I hung back with a niggling suspicion that I was on the menu. Everyone left me alone and disappeared for a few seconds before Andrew came back and led me into a room and we fell onto a large double bed. Aware of the other boys, I felt self-conscious but did not stop him from kissing me on the lips, the door slightly ajar. Until now, no one knew how close we had become, assured none of the other boys would spread the word. I also realized it was the first time I had been on a double bed.

Imagining we were on the grassy field, the soft bed jolted me back to reality and I felt the whole thing was planned. I heard the other boys chatter and laugh, wondering if it was going to be a case of musical kissing chairs. When Andrew was done, he left, and I stayed on the bed, unsure what was going to happen next. I heard someone enter the room and climb onto the bed. The older boy hesitated but looked determined to kiss me. Going through the motions, he kissed me shyly before making a hasty escape and I was on my own again, lips and face flushed and burning. When no one entered after a few seconds, I walked out of the room, only to find everyone had left, except the boy who lived in the huge house. Giddy and confused, I pounded unfamiliar streets before I reached my tiny shack.

The episode had been strange and never to be repeated or mentioned among Andrew, the other boys or myself. Being bullied and kissed was one thing, but allowing groups of boys to kiss you, one after the other, was different. I felt more self-conscious because some of my friends had seen it happen. No one had forced me and neither did I put up much of a fight. Shawn and Andrew, my regular kissing buddies, remained a constant and when I sat back and watched everyone around me, I gravitated towards a tall dark-haired girl in my class. Sharon and I shared the same birthday month, so I joined their group of friends, yet still felt like the odd one out. They looked out for me around the school grounds, and I tried my best to be one of the crowds.

Chapter 23: a shamefaced son and partisan parishioners

I got to spend all four and a half years of primary school living in the tiny shack. Life around the shacks was as colourful as the permanent dwellers and transient individuals. Giving the appearance of a carefree and happy child, I kept my emotions bottled and I found ways to release the tension and pressure when things spiralled out of control. My family and I lived in the tiny shack. It became my haven and a prison cell. Rosie, my older sister, had left school and searched for a job. She kept herself busy by entering local beauty competitions and expanding her social circle, yet we never knew or met any of her friends. No stranger came calling at the shack, even though she was a very pretty girl. Frank, on the other hand, kept to himself and gave nothing away. A group of siblings bound by blood yet so very distant and isolated. My sister struggled to find employment, her lack of schooling a major factor. Most adults did menial jobs in factories, supermarkets or retail stores. Job hunting became a priority, parents did a good job of nagging tirelessly until one was driven out of the house in frustration. Good enough jobs were advertised by word of mouth, with family members looking out for their own before spreading the news further afield.

My brother Frank, the clever one, when not at school spent most or all his time out and about. He came home to eat, bathe and sleep, but we never saw him do any studying or homework. No one questioned him either. Most older boys and young men stood and loitered outside the local shop, smoking, chatting or teasing pedestrians and shoppers.

With downcast eyes, I prayed his presence might discourage them from calling out to me as I ran errands. Whether he smoked or joined them in whatever they did, he was a closed book. Since he caused no trouble, my silent pensive brother was turning into a stranger right before my eyes. Two brothers, one silent and placid by nature, the other silenced and docile in shame.

My dear sweet mother spent most of her day in the shack, keeping it clean and tidy. A visit to her sister, Sophie, who lived close by or other family relatives, provided some reprieve from the confines of our tiny home. Private and reserved, she was happy and comfortable in her little space. Intermittent hospital or church visits were a staple and expected excursion. Dragging her kids along for the ride, I chose the clinic above our Sunday church outings. Sometimes I came home to an empty shack, downing a quick cup of tea, usually black or with spoons of powdered milk, and a bleak sandwich. The homework could wait, and I would lock the door, draw the curtains and hide, enjoying some private time. I let my mind wander and roam, shedding those pent-up tears until none were left. Unbeknown to everyone, I tied flimsy scarves around my waist, head and shoulders, creating fairy tales about my boyfriends as I danced or acted out many scenarios, lost in a world of fantasy.

I twirled, high kicked and pirouetted while trying out some splits on the shiny floor as it took me a while to realize I was never going to be a supple and flexible dancer. The lack of some things would come and haunt me much later. Mind you, I never stopped trying to do the splits.

Sometimes when I felt brave enough, I retraced my mother's footsteps, dodging many bullies and boys, with the hope of getting a better meal after school. Every house she visited appeared to have more to eat and drink than my own. Was it just an illusion for those living in shacks and with no space to pack food? The cupboards seemed to hide food and sweets from us, our ears primed for the sound of creaking doors and the wrappers of sweets and biscuits. To a barefoot kid, hunger pangs were part and parcel of a daily struggle.

The government grant donated to poor families fed and clothed us, barely even, while donations, hand-me-downs and good Samaritans did the rest. Meal options were very limited, alternating from a sandwich to cooked rice and mealie meal – our word for corn seed or maize – the cheapest and longest-lasting choice. Imported by the Portuguese to Africa, it had turned into a staple diet in many African countries. Cooked, the maize was edible for many a day and needed no refrigeration. Mealie meal is like American grits and Italian polenta, made of white instead of yellow maize. Whatever the origin or the preparation, it filled the hunger gaps.

My father had found a gardening space, and his vegetables popped up easily and filled the pots and our stomachs. Sunday meals were the best in most households. Chicken was a staple; red meat was almost a let down on that lunch plate. Meat on a week day was a definite bonus. Pilchards and sardine meals signalled that the bottom of the purse was in sight. A bowl of dry, coarse mealie meal, minus the meat, and mixed with milk was a sure sign money was very tight. On the worst days, cups of sweet black tea with some slices of dry, or if we were lucky, buttered bread with a thin layer of peanut butter or jam and sandwich spread, had to do the trick.

It was unpleasant watching parents battle for provisions to feed kids, come up empty handed and try to sleep without any food in our bellies. My dad would leave early the next morning, hoping to sell vegetables, while I hauled produce back and forth. I was the baby in the home and therefore the elected debt collector of the family. This was one duty I came to hate, instilling deep feelings of helplessness, anger and shame as I was left to loiter and wait for an answer.

So, you understand why visits, especially on a Sunday, to friends or relatives were the preferred options, hoping they never saw the hunger and desperation in our eyes. Our priest may have seen it during Sunday sermons. Raised as Methodists, we had to attend Sunday school and church with our mother. My father never came along, and he made sure to disappear whenever someone from the church happened to pop into our shack.

The worst part, for me, was having to wear a cheap shiny three-piece polyester suit. It felt hot, uncomfortable and made me more self-conscious as we walked to church, the bullies not respecting the day, my mum or older sister. My brother scooted ahead, not always appearing in the pews as he grew older. Sunday school was fun but sermons a long, slow and boring affair. Older kids fidgeted while toddlers ran along aisles, their screams and cries halting and prolonging the services. Our local church was drenched in social class and hierarchy, thanks to the patrons who provided some amusing if not comical diversions.

Kids from the better side of town wore casual comfortable clothes to church and they looked presentable enough. Our parents insisted we dress up in the shiny cheap three-piece suits, mini versions of the male elders seated around us. We sat quietly, behaved yet fighting down yawns and the urge to fidget. The other kids ran amok, ignoring the gentle reprimands from their parents. One look from our parents was good enough to keep one rooted to the wooden pew, sweating and praying the service would end. Not everything was doom and gloom as we sang or mimed the hymns from a frayed hymn book.

Generally, the priest, an elder or the congregation started a hymn and we followed. If someone was unhappy about the pace, generally those from the posher side of town, a battle of tunes ensued. Kids giggled at the disharmony, adults looked around for some order to be restored. Amid titters and mumbling, hymns were stopped and restarted, or we chose a new one to keep the peace. All I wanted to do was race home and take off that ugly shiny suit.

My mother had other plans as she dragged me around to visit relatives along the way. Frank could move on ahead while I tagged along, expectations of some food or sweets soothing my discomfort. I had to keep the suit clean so there was no chance of playing games, not that I planned anyway. The bullies smirked and commented but I remained a silent, overdressed sissy. Perhaps I told myself I would never wear suits as an adult; the discomfort and unwanted attention was something I could do without. Yet, like a dutiful son, I made my way to church, praying for a time when I would be given a choice to stay at home on a Sunday.

My mother was the avid churchgoer, my dad not, and I never gave any thought to their different personalities at the time, much less their education level. Reading some newspaper article to my parents was the norm, but I found out they lacked some basic writing skills. My parents struggled to write their name, much less sign it. Signing my school report was a job delegated to my sister, as I climbed up the academic ladder.

My dear parents were farm born and raised, and our small city, with crowds of strangers in the town centre, sent my mother into a fluster, while my father went into town once every month to collect his disability grant. Despite my shyness and awkwardness, she made sure I led the way and asked questions. My poor parents stumbled over words as they tried to explain, sometimes confusing and misinterpreting things, until their son and daughter took over. Feeling sorry for them, I pushed away the idea I was embarrassed for having uneducated parents, as did many other kids around me. That we lived in a small wooden box called a shack, was an added soul-destroying bonus.

Keeping quiet about my miserable home situation and unhappy social life, I created a presentable and reliable image along the way. I wore a brave face, masking a struggle to soothe my emotional pain, distress and loneliness. My family, a frolicsome school or even a provocative social life, occupied extreme ends of my adolescent years. I did not have long to go before the teenage phase added fuel to the confusing internal fires kept burning by the bullies and suitors.

Chapter 24: making a friend and reaching out

My friendship with Irwin was confined to school and I had no idea what he did after we parted at his gate. He always spoke about some girl who was never going to look in his direction, but he harboured the crush anyway. I was not sure if we spoke about my situation, but I had no interest in girls, happily enjoying the attention of my many little suitors. Was I going through a phase and snap out of it at some later date? I felt fraudulent but comfortable around the girls, awkward and suspicious among groups of boys. Verbally pummelled and physically mauled from all directions, I ran away as the bullies chased me, and found a new friend in the process. The alliance felt strange at first, yet calming as I tried to spread my wings, remaining introverted and reserved.

Sharon's house was along the school route, and I used it as an escape route and later as the place to study and do homework. She was not as diligent as her quiet friend and left it all for the last minute, while I studied and read weeks in advance. The adrenaline rush and scramble to cram before a test or exam was not for me. Somehow, it felt easy and relaxed in her family home, and I became the silent boy on the couch. Our birthdays a few days apart, Sharon was as talkative and outgoing as I was silent and shy. She was the one to hop around in class, sharing notes, revising or copying homework.

Surrounded by a group of friends, they welcomed me into the fold, saving me from a bunch of marauding tormentors. The boys were not going to pick a fight with girls, so I secretly called her my friend. I was unsure how they felt about me. Questions or any mention of my perceived orientation would never surface. I enjoyed feeling as though I was part of a group, tagging along for the ride, offering wisdom, aid and homework as the levy for the inclusion. Joining the social games at home and school, I was unpolished when it came to interact as a friend, since no one really treated me as one. I was to be a follower and never the leader among my so-called friends. I was a tense ball of nerves once surrounded by groups of kids, all watching to see where or how I fit into the scheme of things. Afraid to attract attention, not to mention living a sad and very boring life, I kept quiet and let them dictate my mood, emotions and actions. A boy liked by girls and loved by the boys, yet hated by the bullies, I was a quivering mess on the inside.

Trying not to feel like an intruder, I became a regular visitor at Sharon's house, sitting upright on the couch. I sat, acted and behaved calmly while hiding my nerves and the discomfort I felt. I answered questions, and conversations were a blur while I stayed quiet and over time, the awkward silence disappeared. Feeling relaxed and accepted as part of the furniture, it felt good sitting on a real couch, watching my friend's family act so differently from my own.

Once seated, I seldom left the house, even after homework was completed. Joining all games created a stir and argument when I was allocated to a team. No one wanted me on their team, so I often sat inside, listening to the screams and laughter while I shared cups of tea with Sharon's mother, Aunt Rhona, as we all knew her.

I kept Aunt Rhona company as she dabbled around the house, both comfortable with my silence and the odd chatter. A good kindhearted soul, she did her best to give and provide for her family. Under present circumstances, we all struggled, some worse than others, of course, but our parents did what they could. Despite not recalling any conversations, I was left alone on the couch, visitors shocked to find a quiet boy on his own. Excusing myself before dinner, I was asked to stay and join in the meal. I tried to leave early as a rule; that extra meal was always welcomed. If I came home early and alive, I gave my parents no reason to question my comings and goings.

Things changed slightly for the better when television sets cropped up in some of the homes. Arriving in South Africa in 1976, they created mixed reactions from our then political leaders. A modern item, though not desirable, it was a spiritual and physical danger to people and would allow the country to import films depicting racial mixing and advertising, which could may make non-white Africans dissatisfied with their lot. They worried that the box from the devil would spread immorality and communism among a people divided by racial laws and prohibitions.

Homes with television sets became popular, as groups of barefoot kids congregated to stare at the black and white screens in fascination. Radio stories were relegated to the back seat as we jostled and argued over a seat on the floor. We were not meant to sit on the couch or settee. Fake friendships bloomed, bribes and battles raged near or outside the door. Stumbling over each other for the best seat, noisy fights broke out and everyone got thrown out for good measure. We raced around the place, hoping to catch the last few minutes of a television show. It was fun being desperate, persistent and poor in the seventies and for a few minutes we forgot about our troubles, amazed at the comedians, fairy tales, drama and animated stories played out on the screen.

My new friend's home sported a television set and I had front seat since I spent most of my time there, even if all the other kids played outside. Most television sets were switched on around six in the afternoon, starting a mass migration to doors. Begging for a seat or told to come back after supper, one sat alone while everyone ate out of sight. There were always many kids around Sharon's home, the television set a big drawing card. I sat quietly, they stared or teased me, amused by my girlish reactions. Warren, a tall dark-skinned boy, took extra pleasure in starting a round of playful tormenting. He reminded me of Shawn and I did enjoy, if not flirt as best I could. Indignant yet pleased at the attention, I pushed him away as everyone sat and played along. Flustered, blushing and shy, the private thoughts belied my obvious physical agitation.

Warren waited for a chance to pounce when no adult was in the room. Hands grabbed at me, pinning me to the couch as he kissed, pulled and pinched me. Muffled voices and laughing floated around as I fought in vain. Rough hands grabbed and bruised my skin and I had no idea why they had to be so cruel and mean. Strangely enough, I felt a quiver of discomfort and excitement, which baffled me even more. It was not a long wait for me to become the centre of attention once again. Before, during and after our school bell rang, I was hounded around the shacks and homes. I got pulled aside while others watched, joined in and mocked me. There was no escape, but I would not allow them to hound me out of the room.

The scene was the same. A posse of boys waited for my arrival or trickled in after me and during commercial breaks I became the entertainment. My aloofness added a tiny display of ardour and aggression heaped onto me.

Gentleness was not part of the core factor when it came to my humiliation on this day. I found them at the gate, the door was closed, and it was too late to make a run for it. Bargaining and begging, I was stepped forward, skittish and ready to bolt. As I neared the door, they surged and lunged for me. Hands dragged me onto the sand and grassy patch before I could make a sound, a hand covered my mouth and all hell broke loose.

My clothes, skin and body were at their mercy, the hand over my mouth was replaced by lips, kissing and biting at the same time. Hands and feet pinned down, I fought the mass of bodies above me, trying to breathe and not panic. There were too many and I was no match for them. The noise must have alerted someone because no one noticed the door open and the angry voice tell them to get off the child.

Bodies scattered and fled in all directions, leaving me gasping and fighting for air in a state of shame, covered in dirt and dust. Laughter echoed as I stumbled into the house to recover my composure, the tears of shame begging to flow. A reprimand was about as much as they got, claiming it was fun, teasing and a game. Others felt I deserved to be shamed and dragged into the sand. No one cared how I felt or asked how I became the boy everyone wanted to demean and humiliate. Embarrassed for being different, I decided it was easier to keep my mouth shut or things would or could only get worse. Well, as my luck would have it, they did.

Chapter 25: Part 1; a timid outsider, looking in

In the semi-darkness, the little boy heard the rustling of blankets as his mother got out of her single bed and came towards him. She had to step over his brother who was fast asleep on the floor. Curled up under the blankets, he felt her hand on his tiny shoulder, nudging him for a response. She whispered the time, a soft reminder that he should get up and go to the shop. Aware she would not leave him alone until he gave a response, he shifted and heard her return to her own single bed. The little boy could smell his father's feet, instantly turning to face the wall which earned him another soft hiss from his mother. It was futile to prolong the torture: being the baby of the family, it was his duty to run and buy fresh milk and bread for the day.

Stretching his body and blinking in the darkness, his eyes adjusted to the faded floral wallpaper, fighting the desire to stay under the warm blankets. Mother and son played out the morning ritual as his father and siblings slept just a few feet away. Trying not to disturb his father, fast asleep and snoring next to him, he hopped over the foot end of the single bed they shared. Taking into consideration their tiny sleeping quarters, uneven wooden flooring, his father's loud snoring and the bouts of coughing, he was sure not a single person had a good night's rest. His sleeping pattern left much to be desired, a problem which would haunt him as he grew older. He could never understand why or how the racking cough and snoring episodes miraculously calmed down at sunrise!

The linoleum floor cover felt cold under his feet as he stepped over his brother asleep on the floor, using a thin foam mattress as a bed. A few extra minutes in bed could be the reward if he did the job quickly, so he put on his shorts and vest, grabbed the few coins on the wooden table and slipped out the shack door. Wiping sleepy eyes, the boy squinted at the scary shadows and silhouettes, took a deep breath and, fighting down the panic, left the safety of the yard, telling himself that the dark images around him were harmless.

The local shop was not too far, and he prepared himself to sprint as fast as he could, a race to beat the shadows and waiting dogs or mongrels who heard his pounding steps from a mile away, not to mention his fear. The boy disturbed their sleep so perhaps it was payback. Some kids were known to throw stones at the dogs, galling and goading them for a response, before racing away in mock horror. One dirty mongrel waited at the gate as if on call, and the kids of the house often set the dog on the boy, only because he was a sissy. The little child feared the dog, knowing that when it barked and charged, it alerted the other dogs to investigate and give chase.

Heart beating wildly, he tried to outrun them, stopping to kick at them or reach for the closest weapon, a stone or stick. Sometimes a voice in the dark alerted the dogs to stand back, but usually he was left to fend for himself. After the discordant barking, it was a relief to reach the shop minus a dog bite. There was still the return trip, but for now, he faced another milestone. Breathing hard, he stepped on the cemented patio of the shop, seeing the older man waiting near the door, shouting out greetings to people passing along the gravel road.

His heart notched up some extra beats as the man smiled at him, watching him come closer, but the boy stopped a few feet away. Expecting the man to turn and walk into the shop, he merely stepped aside for the child to enter. They both knew the drill as it had been played out many times before. He was not going into the shop until the man went behind the counter. Cars raced by as they stared at one another, the crunching of footsteps on loose stones sounding louder in the near darkness.

The boy had to decide, should he enter and face the inevitable alone or wait until they had an audience. He told no one about being humiliated early in the morning nor did he mention anything about enjoying what was done to him, but minus the audience of course. Before he decided what to do, the man turned and walked into the shop and it seemed as if he would be spared this morning. Warily, he followed as the man asked him what he needed. The usual cheap carton of milk and fresh bread was his reply. A sudden turn and the man lunged at the boy, his strong brown hands pulling him closer and pushed him against the wall. Screaming, fighting or begging would be pointless, but the child struggled anyway, putting up the front in case someone entered the shop while praying no one did. The taller male pinned the smaller boy to the wall and eyes made brief contact before he dropped his head as if to kiss the boy.

Shaking his head from side to side, he begged the man to let him go but was ignored, and felt the darker lips settle and nibble at his exposed neck. He tensed, worried about any marks on his fair skin. Pleading not to be left with a love bite, he felt the hairs on his neck tickle and prickle. Their simple game of cat and mouse long gone and forgotten, the boy relaxed and allowed Ronald to finish what he had started. They stood like lovers, the older man kissing the boy as if he was a girl, aware that anyone might enter the shop and find them but confident enough to know he was doing what all the others did, mocking the sissy. No one did stop him, in fact they merely watched until it reached humiliating point and Ronald felt the boy had suffered enough. There was no rush, it seemed, as Ronald wrapped his arms around the boy and cuddled him closer.

The boy surrendered and relaxed his body, fighting the urge to sigh at the feeling. He felt they were doing the right thing, so why did he feel the older man tense? Or was it his imagination or anxiety at the thought of being caught and ridiculed? Fighting the urge to purr, his mind buzzed at the image they created and his mixed emotions. The older man assumed the boy hated his touch and would never know the truth. Riddled with a bunch of mixed emotions, he kept his eyes closed when Ronald stopped, but kept him pinned to the wall. Did he sense the change, or had he done enough for the morning?

Opening his eyes, the child stared back at the dark irises above him, wondering what would follow. Ronald suddenly moved away and walked behind the counter to find a loaf of bread and milk, putting it on the counter. Wordlessly, he paid and grabbed the items. Dismissed, he walked away, disappointed and relieved as he raced home, face, neck and body flushed from the kissing. Fleeing the barking dogs, the adrenaline rush made him fearless.

Too excited to hop back into bed, he set about starting the day. Was he being used by Ronald even though he enjoyed being kissed? In the morning he was gentle and kind to the boy, except when he had an audience to play to. Aggressive and forceful, it felt like he was being punished for being the sissy. Nestled between a rock and hard place every morning, he knew things could go either way. Ronald waiting at the door was a good sign but when stationed behind the counter, everything went askew for the child everyone knew as David.

Chapter 25: part two; a barefoot walk to misery and shame

David walked along the semi-tarred street, looking down, ignoring the voices around him. They knew he heard every word, taunt and insinuation. Hands tried to touch and grab him, screams reminding them he was dirty and filthy, not to be touched. He could not tell them Ronald and some other boys touched, kissed and held him; it would add more fuel to the fire, so he gritted his teeth and soldiered on. David knew the truth, but he sadly had no one to share it with. Tucking the hurtful out of sight yet not out of his mind, he fought to keep the tears from falling down his cheeks

They said he walked, talked, and acted like a girl. Mentally his many little boyfriends expected it from him. David knew his mannerisms were affected or different, because they told him and pushed him into the girls' corner. Reminded he was not really one of them, everyone laughed along, at and with him. Light-hearted teasing or fun-filled moments were far and few between as they shunted him from pillar to post, an outcast, intermittently allowed into their world when the need arose.

Running daily walks of shame was pure torture. "You act like a girl, you sissy," one proclaimed. "You a moffie—gay boy," another reminded him in case he forgot. They ignored the adults who admonished them, intent on shaming David, whose tiny chest constricted in shame, frustration and misery. Out of spite, they set dogs after him and others tried to take the shopping money off him. Sometimes they did, gloating while he begged. "You even want to cry like a girl," they chanted before flinging the money at him and a few kids ran away, bored or satisfied by the reaction. Drowning out the malicious voices, he recited the purchases in his head as he walked towards the shop.

The tarred road became a gravel and sandy path riddled with potholes, and he hopped over the uneven surfaces. After heavy rains, the potholes filled with water and were a perfect tool to splash each other when least expected, and David was no exception. It was no fun running errands or going to and from school with wet clothing, shoes and socks. Nearing the shop, he prayed they would leave him alone. When they noticed a group of older boys gathered around the shop corner and entrance, his bullies fell back out of fear or respect. The unwritten rule in the township.

These older boys smoked, chatted, joked or annoyed passing pedestrians. Sometimes they took his side, getting the bullies off his back, and he hoped today they would do the same. Nonetheless, groups of boys, old or young, made him apprehensive as they watched him approach. Stony-faced and anxious, the shop door seemed miles away as he heard someone pass a comment, followed by peals of laughter and cheering. David didn't see the hand reach out and grab his arm until it was too late. Jerked and pulled into the circle of older boys, he instinctively tightened his body, eyes downcast, knowing that a fight would be pointless. There was a strange smell in the air and he looked at the boy who held his arm in a tight grip, the glazed eyes smiling back, and David knew he was in trouble. Frozen in fear, his eyes begged for mercy or to be released.

The smell of marijuana, weed, grass or dagga as we knew it, hung in the air, and David waited for the boy to make a move, but he seemed hesitant for some reason. Looking in the direction they faced, his heart sank and prayed they would let him go, sparing him another bout of disgrace and shame. People walked by, some glancing their way, eyes filled with disgust or pity, yet no one saw the scared and panicked look in the eyes of the smaller boy. A few seconds later, David was pushed against the wall amid cheers and his captor leaned closer, teasing him with a promise of freedom if he obeyed. The fun was about to start, and he heard the nervous snicker, daring the older boy to go through with whatever he planned to do, "Please don't; let me go," he begged softly, a silent prayer offered to be spared a painful public experience. There was a determined expression on the face of the boy staring back at him. David observed the tanned face dappled with youthful facial hair come closer. Lighter brown eyes met darker ones as the taller boy, no older than seventeen, smirked and brought his lips closer. David had no intention of being kissed and turned his head to the side.

Lips grazed his neck and a set of teeth bit into his soft skin and laughter erupted at the boy's audacity. David shut his eyes, blocking out the shame, aware pedestrians had an idea what was going on. As the smell of weed invaded his nostrils, he hoped a good Samaritan would come to his rescue. His captor released his arms but kept his body hostage and pinned to the wall. They resembled young lovers, leaning up against the wall, and yet no one saw anything wrong with the picture. Did David like it, since there was little resistance? Martin dropped his head to kiss, lick and bite David's neck.

Of course, David liked it. Only he knew that, and it was his secret. He hated it when it became a game to them, and he a body devoid of emotions or feelings. Ridiculing and blasting him for being effeminate, they never saw that he was also a human being, and still a little child at that. David had no one on his side, or any idea how to express what he felt. It was very confusing and exciting at the same time. Surrounded, he had never felt so alone, knowing that everyone had a public glimpse into his secret pain.

Martin stopped his licking, made brief eye contact with David and kissed him full on the lips. The sheer boldness made him open his mouth in shock, but the semi-drugged Martin mistook the signal and pushed his tongue between the lips, deepening the kiss.

For the first time, David felt the tears tickle his eyelashes and tried to push Martin off him. The older boy shoved him harder into the wall and kissed him roughly. The pain and embarrassment gave him extra strength as Martin stumbled backwards. His troop clapped at the show of defiance which annoyed or infuriated him. He lunged at David and forced his tongue back into position. This time the kissing was crude and harsh; it was meant to hurt and belittle. Martin rubbed his bigger body into the smaller one and David heard people laughing, whistling and clapping at them.

The assault in his lips lasted a few seconds before the older boy stopped and moved a step back. David took deep breaths hoping it was all over. Staring at his aggressor, he may have misjudged the satisfaction or slivers of disgust? He looked down at his feet while Martin joined his friends. No one came to his side, as he sunk down against the wall, hugging his knees. Shivering and holding back the tears,

Martin was praised for putting the sissy boy in his place. Others teased him, but he said the weed made me do it.

His skin hot and feeling bruised, David rose from the wall, watching in case someone else made a grab at him. Luckily, they had their fun and left him like most of the other boys, used and left to deal with the aftermath. The story of his life and whether it was a stolen kiss or a public diversion, the twisted emotions of guilt, shame or pleasure all blended into one dark ball of confusion. It seemed no one wanted to let him be a sissy in peace.

David walked towards the shop door, the concrete flooring cold under his bare feet. It was tough keeping the tears at bay, but he was determined. Ignoring a gloating crowd, he never saw some the eyes and faces filled with pity, assuming everyone gloated and relished his public debasement. He heard a familiar voice and felt his skin flush some more as his heart blazed and shattered into a million pieces. No one would understand the intense agony he experienced before he walked through the shop door.

Chapter 25: part three; a very public humiliation

David shivered, too scared to look in the direction of the voice even though he had no reason to do so. He knew they watched him and he felt compelled to look up, only to see another pair of light brown eyes staring back at him. The blank stare was just that, yet concealed revulsion and disgust, or something close to that. Was he projecting his own feelings into the eyes of his brother Frank? David found it hard to believe his older brother had watched the entire scene and never come to his rescue.

Realizing why the boys hesitated for a few seconds after they grabbed him, they were unsure of Frank's reaction. They might not have bothered because we were strangers, a pair of boys related by the genetic pool. His own brother ignored him for being gay or a sissy. Entering the shop, humiliation washed over him as the voices, walls, the floor and people blended into a big fuzzy ball. Blacking everything out, David huddled into self-preservation mode whenever he felt very insecure, self-conscious and the centre of attention.

Keeping his head down, he stood in line against the wall, waiting to be served. David never saw Ronald watch him and smile as the shop filled with customers and beggars. The gave him space and everyone inched forward as others got served. He could taste the marijuana in his mouth. The urge to spit was great, but he prayed his voice was not going to be high-pitched and girlish. That usually caused bouts of laughter and taunts. Gulping down the vile taste, he looked up and placed his order, but the man asked him to speak up.

Repeating himself, the man spitefully ignored him and said, "Ronald, come and serve your girlfriend" and turned to the next customer. Everyone giggled except David and a smiling Ronald appeared to aid his girlfriend. Collecting the items at leisure, he had a knack for making small talk to people in the shop, while whispering to the little boy at the counter, almost intimately, yet loud enough for the others to hear. David had an urge to run out of the shop but a trip to another shop would have had the same outcome, if not worse.

Ronald held out his hand for the money, but David placed the coins on the counter. He reached out for the cheap plastic bag, but someone shoved it away from him. He gave a silent plea for Ronald to stop the charade, but he only stared back at the boy he kissed almost every morning. Did he imagine the pity in those dark eyes? Ronald offered the bag to his little friend, who never saw the hairy arm and hand reach and grip his wrist. David tried to break free, but someone stood behind him and held him prisoner just as Ronald let him go. Ordering his accomplice to hold on to the boy, David watched the tall figure walk around the counter, poised to assert his power and his heart sank into his barefoot feet once again.

People scattered, giving Ronald some space as the older boy pulled David closer and started to kiss his neck. Pulling away in shock, Ronald pushed him against the wall as a shop full of people watched him hold and kiss the boy like it was a natural thing to do. His lips trailed the boy's neck, lips and mouth as they did some mornings, but this time, it felt very different.

Suffering the same public indignity twice in a short space of time, while his older and distant brother loitered outside, David felt the fight leave his body. Ronald stopped to look at him, noticed the hurt and pleading in the eyes yet kept him close. He dipped a bit and resumed kissing his girlfriend while everyone applauded his actions. Funny or strange, David was deeply hurt at the public humiliation, but no one knew how hard it was to maintain the inner peace and joy he felt when someone held and kissed him. It was the only thing that stopped him from breaking down and exposing his weakness.

A voice encouraged Ronald to give him a love bite, but he only laughed at the demand. Knowing his brother may be outside, listening to them, was a mental image too hard or painful to bear. "Why are you doing this to me?" he whispered to Ronald but got no reply. His darker eyes conveyed it was just a game, a teasing one at that. It was not a joke at all, but the boy felt he was being mocked. Finally, Ronald stepped back and handed over the bag and David walked out of the shop, gingerly expecting someone to pull him back. The boys had done it before, wanting to please Ronald and earn favours. David, shoulders dropped in rejection and misery, walked home. Even the dogs left him alone, sensing his shame and broken soul. The kids never let him off, demanding to know if he liked being a sissy and kissing the boys. He fought the urge to scream back, "Yes, I do like it a lot, so what?" Choosing to remain silent and defiant, he ignored everyone, yet they made him wonder what if it had been one of them in his shoes? How would they cope or handle the harassment?

He hoped there were no marks on him and gave some lame excuse for taking so long. Walking out of the shack, he crossed the road and made his way into the forest to find a suitable place among the tall grass and trees. Pondering the last encounter, his body grew hot with shame and confusion. Rolling onto his belly he felt waves of pity and a deep sense of utter loneliness. He could not fight the tears as they leaked out, silent at first, onto the grass underneath him. Before long, his body jerked as if in agony as the suppressed anguish and heartache boiled to the fore. Among the birds, butterflies and insects, he cried his little heart out. Being a child, he did not fully understand the term isolation and loneliness as an emotional or social response. His tears soothed most of the intense, agonizing and confusing feelings away.

When he had no tears left, he slunk home, passing the scavenging dogs, cats and mice along the way. Stepping over broken glass, rubbish, and nettles, eyes red and swollen, no one made a fuss over him. It was obvious David had been crying but kids cried for many reasons back then. If there were no blood stains or torn clothing, it was a given that someone had a fight. David explained it away before hopping into bed. Faced with a wooden wall, his back near his dad's feet, he mulled over everything before the lure of sleep beckoned. Time. Sometimes the misery overshadowed his little moments of merriment.

As he drifted to sleep, David had no idea he would be subjected to the same treatment daily for the next few years. There would be a shift in the intensity and variation of the

201

degradation as he grew older. Ronald in the morning was a stark contrast to the person he faced during the day. After the Martin episode, most of the older boys tried their luck, and the verbal vitriol remained a constant, reminding him he was filthy and the sissy no one liked. With time, he created an internal happy space when things became too much. Sadly, it came at a time when the damage had already been done. Alone and shunned, David created his own coping mechanisms, unaware that they would come back to haunt him in the future.

A few people might have had an idea what David went through at school, the shop or around the house. From around the age of eight, he grew a thick skin when faced with strangers or sometimes friends who belittled and called him rude names, shouting out obscenities in his direction because he liked other boys. Going about his daily duties, he was treated like someone with a contagious illness, yet he hurt no one. Timid, shy and quiet, he protected a fragile yet tenacious child-like acceptance of what and who he was. No one was going to take that from him. The boys kissed an extroverted and frivolous David, yet to his primary school classmates, he was the very introverted and studious, yet reserved boy they called Georgie.

Chapter 26: sociable relations and roguish drivers

I never thought it odd, but we were all in primary school after relocating. Rosie and I were born in 1961 and 1967 respectively. It appears she may have missed some years of schooling, sharing a class with her brother born three years after her. Outgoing, pretty and friendly, she was nothing like her brothers. Frank was the quiet, almost antisocial one, silently moving about the place, only speaking when the need arose. I, the tiny brother, was a ball of confusion, crunching down any social spontaneity to be a wallflower, blending into the background, silenced by bullies and tagged a 'freak.'

Despite everyone being aware of my practices away from the shack, not once did any family member or relative bring up the topic of my unmanly mannerisms or attitude. I was David, the sissy boy to friends and suitors and Georgie, a teased and bullied class friend. I was merely a son and brother to my family, no one called me out for being a social misfit behind the bolted shack door. That my brother had caught me with a boy, and witnessed my shame and public humiliation, and never came to my rescue, added to my anxiety around family and relatives.

Bullied, ostracized outside the shack while being worried, scared and mentally distant around the home, gives a bleak impression of my life. Yet when a suitor led me away to a private hideout, held and kissed me, all the misery and ache melted away. The bullying words and names faded as I revelled in being treated like a girl, wanting the kisses to last forever. In the boys' arms, I felt like a girl, I reacted like one, giving a false sense of acceptance to the boy who was never going to be or think like me. They told me everything wrong with the physical picture, yet in my head and heart, it was a perfect image. Emotionally and physically accepting the path I had chosen or been directed into, braving it in public was going to take many years.

Those solo forays into the forest allowed me to reflect on everything, venting feelings to birds, bees and trees around me. I let out my feelings of dejection, shedding tears of inner pain, loneliness, isolation, and rejection, while my head and heart struggled to find some happy place before facing the world again.

Mope not, I said, and there were some happy moments around the shack when my mother's sister visited from time to time, as she did in our first brick home. Like most transient visitors, I had no idea where she came from and returned to or might have forgotten. Aunt Trina was always welcome and very different from her sister. Brown-eyed and a shade darker in skin tone, she was also taller and extroverted compared to her shorter, quiet, and shy green-eyed sister. Spoiling us with a tasty cooked meal or sweet things, she flitted in and out of our lives over the years we spent in the shack.

She always wore 'crimplene slacks,' even though people said she had lovely legs. My mother hated the mere mention of the word, preferring softer, pastel flower embossed chiffon-like dresses, skirts and blouse sets. Crimplene or polyester cloth originated in the 1950's and was named after the Crimple Valley in Harrogate, North Yorkshire. It was a heavy, wrinkle-free cloth with a permanently pressed look. Although crimplene raced out of fashion during the 1970's in Britain, back in my hood in South Africa, the elder set rocked a single or twin set crimplene outfit. Apparently, these now dated fashion items were called the working man's outing clothes.

Aunt Trina, as far as we knew, had never married, and when she visited, another foam mattress on the wooden flooring meant there was no space to move about once we had all settled into bed. Stepping and climbing over each other, a trip to the outside toilet or a penny spent in the round plastic bucket kept at the door, became an obstacle course. It continued for nine years and finally, I know the reasons for my bad sleeping patterns or the insomnia I suffer from as an adult. The lack of privacy and space, nightly disturbances, the noises and sounds, intensified in the near dark and small condensed shacks, all added to a distorted sleeping schedule. I still have not found a cure for my insomnia, despite knowing or justifying the causes, and I continue to suffer because of my past.

When Aunt Trina dragged along a suitor and moved into an adjoining shack, it felt like I had another mother to care for and feed us. Her partner, Uncle James, was a subdued man until he had a drink or two. Garrulous and funny, we laughed at his antics, while Aunt Trina tried to keep him in line. No amount of her coaxing or scolding did the trick. Bickering long into the night, we all dreaded the weekends and his funny drunken antics. With relief and sadness, they would relocate, only to return and repeat the cycle, until he disappeared from our lives completely. Aunt Trina would maintain her nomadic existence, remaining a distant figure throughout my life as a child though less as I grew into a young adult, often disappearing for many years at a time.

Her brother, my Uncle Reginald, the male version and image of my mother, came from Cape Town, they said. With a loud booming voice, jocular and funny, sober or not, he turned the yard into a good-humored party zone. Inviting everyone to join and drink, his jokes and chatter became darker and dirtier, as we giggled while adults tried to rein in his behaviour. A semi-drunk and boisterous uncle Reginald was fair game for a few pennies as we played bartender and, much later, a shoulder to lean on. We missed his antics and favours while adults were happy for the peace and quiet he left behind.

Their father, my grandfather, Atoor Kok and Aunt Trina always visited us at the same time. He was short and used a walking stick to move about, his back slightly hunched over. Facially he resembled my mother, uncle and aunt, except he had a much darker skin tone, like a roasted almond. Unlike his son, he was laid back and quiet, with slow, measured speech, as if trying to make you understand his words. My dad and grandfather would spend hours chatting in the shade, if they were not listening to the little transistor radio beside them. They bonded over vegetable patches and it was one of the few times I saw my father comfortable and relaxed. Of course, he was the son-in-law, but he was almost a stranger to me as a kid. With the understanding that he went back to Cape Town, there were no set dates for a return or follow-up visit by Atoor.

Unlike the annual farm excursions to my dad's place of birth and meeting relatives on his side of the family, we never took a trip to this place called Cape Town, only meeting family members from my mother's side when they came around. These sporadic visits meant I had little or no background about my mum's childhood. Not that I knew much in the first place. My grandparents from both sides are faint, elusive figures from childhood. Their short visits hardly gave us time to bond, question, or probe the past, not that it was the thing to do at any time. Kids were not meant to ask impertinent questions, and if they did pass on any information, it faded from my memory over the years. Without too much being given away at this stage, it would be easier to cry defeat in feeding you a more detailed account of my family tree and their traits.

Who knows what the future chapters might hold but for now it is safe to say both my parents, grandparents and many relatives are a total mystery to me. This became clear when I started writing the book; probing questions gave even less or no information. I do promise to try and fill the gaps as I write, and you read along in-patient anticipation and, hopefully, pleasure.

Perhaps I must bite the bullet, going back to dig up roots and unearth a rich and wonderful intriguing history which may have smouldered and fluttered out of reach. That it may have added a bigger story line to my memoir and perhaps my life, saddens me greatly, as I have no idea as to this possibility.

My woeful family history aside, peripatetic relatives were not the only ones infusing our humdrum lives with excitement. Long- and short-term shack dwellers all became a big happy family over weekends, especially payday. Bills were settled amongst them and everyone proceeded to party like there was no tomorrow. Loud music, dancing, eating and intoxicated voices continued until early morning. Kids acted as waiters, butlers or messengers. Stray dogs, cats and dishevelled greedy kids fought for every scrap and morsel around the place.

Whether it was fun, games, tricks or pranks, we forgot about the hard existence, making the most of every day. With our meagre meals, threadbare clothing and scraping the bottom of the financial barrel for most of the month, we enjoyed and appreciated the smallest or simplest things and activities around the home and in the community. The odd holier-than-thou neighbours tried keeping things toned down and respectable, which worked for short periods before alcoholic drinks flowed. Older people and most shack visitors enjoyed the bitter-tasting cheap home-made maize alcoholic drink, while the younger set enjoyed guvine or guveen, as they pronounced it.

Originally a German homemade wine called Glühwein, those who drank it got drunk, incoherent, argumentative or easily manipulated to open a purse string. Stronger than the maize drink, arguments broke out over a lost, stolen, or misplaced bottle of guveen. Sharing drinks with a friend stretched as far as they watched the speed of your intake, often hiding bottles out of sight. Not everything was shared, some favours not always politely reciprocated, yet every poor person and household got their time in the limelight.

Visits to the town centre were usually announced in advance, so we bragged about the excursion, becoming a pariah or best friend. One wore the best item of clothing as we stared at everything in sight. Everything looked expensive, as our poor parents picked and pondered over goods to match the money in their purses and pockets. Hanging on to a hand, arm, leg or clothing item for dear life, it was no wonder white kids stared at us confidently and smugly, with a hint of disdain. White shopkeepers and owners and their sales people were often blatantly rude, abrupt or impatient to our self-conscious, ill-dressed and clumsy parents.

From a young age I got to know that white shop people judged us by skin colour, the way we spoke, dressed, behaved and of course, the amount of money we spent. Mostly, the latter served you well until it was safely deposited into the cash register, their fake smiles vanishing the minute you left the door. The underlying and imposed dynamics of business, banter, barter and cultural bonding across the colour line were still years away. For now, it was important to look decent, be polite while you hand over your cash and race out of sight and out of town. They had no idea how much hassle it took to get there, be treated like a leper while spending our money, and returning home.

We, the poverty-stricken masses, depended on public transport for the odd rambling into town. A dismal bus service jolted along our streets and roads, collecting passengers from across the huge forest. Watching its progress in excitement, we raced to our nearest stop, frustrated and annoyed as the bus sped past, leaving us covered in clouds of dust. There were days when an almost empty bus went by and another where there was no space, but the driver encouraged people to make space. Irate men and women berated unsporting drivers and passengers alike, the pleasurable short bus ride turning into a noisy hell.

Alternatively, we used the taxi service at hand. It was nothing like the cab services of today, may I add. Back then, anyone with a car and time on their hands turned into a taxi to make extra cash. Taxi sign exhibited or not, we all piled into a stranger's car as it sped back and forth along the dusty roads, escorting locals around, making the most of the useless bus timetable, convinced that only two buses serviced our area. Our helpful local drivers, many known by name or sight, allowed us to fill any type of car along the routes. Shopping stuffed into the boot, or piled on laps, on the floor, taxis were filled to the brim by greedy car owners and drivers. Many shopping bags meant you were ignored or encouraged to force yourself into an already crowded car. Let me just mention that this included body sizes of all descriptions and leave it at that.

The driver huddled three or four passengers into the front, piling as many as he could in the back seats. With someone straddling the gear stick, the odd lurch or zigzag elicited screams of panic and astonishment at the nerve and audacity, but also their anger for allowing it to happen. Buried under shopping and squashed tightly into doors and seats, one could only pray for travel mercies. As passengers alighted, kids or shopping were passed from lap to lap to make space for newcomers. Since most passengers carried similar shopping bags, items went missing, purposely or not. Drivers spent the suitable amount of time soothing an angry passenger, promising nothing really because there was no lost, found and return service among the poor.

Not all taxis were in the best of condition, nor were most drivers properly licensed to drive any car for that matter. Jerking from side to side, erratic swerving assured us the driver might be under the influence of weed or alcohol – the smell of both giving us a short pause for concern, the need to accomplish an errand overriding sensibility. If the driver was clearly a hazard, the brave remained while the sensible passengers insisted on changing rides. There was never a dull moment along the badly potholed roads and streets.

Over time, we knew which taxis or drivers to avoid since they became a major source of transport as the years meandered along. We used, supported and abused each other in the process and despite our frustrating trips, we lived to tell some tales. Before taxi laws and regulations, getting around in the 70's and early 80's was exasperating, tense and challenging, yet no one bothered much about the dangers of getting into a strange or stranger's car.

Chapter 27: a scenic ramble regarding sparse provisions

As I hobbled up the primary school ladder, many crude shacks were nailed and bolted into place around our neighbourhood and surrounding forest. With only a government income, many of us were going nowhere in a hurry. Yards were filled with shacks, the extra cash used to extend or improve the main brick house in the yard, often with fewer occupants than the tiny shacks behind them, the irony lost among the rotating maids, factory workers and workers from afar who needed a short-term place to stay, unlike a few who overstayed their welcome, becoming part of the location, or township.

Conscious that mixed or bi-racial is the new politically and socially correct term to use, I will continue to use the term 'coloured' as stated on my birth certificate. I feel that it sounds natural and easier to visualize as I write, but I apologies to those readers who find the word offensive or insulting.

Coloured was the term used by the then-white South African government during the apartheid era to create a racially divided society, separating us from whites, Indians and blacks in the country. Due to our generous ancestral pool, physical features among a group of people or families were distinctive or different. We were a varied mixture of skin tones or colours, facial features, different accents and character traits, naturally.

Ancestral genetics or bloodlines did not favour all siblings, as we ranged from having very fair, pale, different shades of olive, tanned to dark brown and pitch-black skin. A common set of brown or black eyes paled alongside a pair of envied blue, grey, green and hazel eyes. Hair textures greatly separated the straight and glossy from the curly, kinky or coarse; we knew it as 'kroes,' a Dutch surname. Black and brown was the norm for most hair colours, with the odd blonde and red head thrown in for a dose of jealousy or bullying. Freckles or shit splatters upped your bullying status, while it was not strange to see an albino child or two in the community.

As you can see, we were a colourful bunch indeed with the misfortune of being under a government hell-bent on moulding us into something they could control. Born with no silver spoon in my mouth, I was an innocent being, raised by parents who accepted their lot as meted out by the government of the day. From where I lived and played, there were not many silver spoons dangling from any mouths. All I saw were people living in small homes and shacks, struggling to make ends meet from one day to the next. This never put much of a damper on our social and cultural status as 'coloured.'

Kids with straight glossy hair and coloured irises were idolized or detested as they ran about flicking heads and necks, showcasing the fluidity of their locks. Enviously admired by those who needed a hurricane to blow a strand of hair out of place, there was some payback when industrial-strength hair straightening creams became popular and used to gain maximum, but short term, admiration and compliments. With my curly head of hair, I was stuck in the middle but too busy fending off bullies and suitors to bother if my hair moved or not.

The other areas close to our neighbourhood were Pefferville, my primary school base, and Parkside, the infamous Durban Flats precinct, with no flats in sight, ironically, and

Parkridge, a section of the latter known as 'Look at me' by the locals. Not sure how or why, since most front doors opened a few steps onto the streets, roads and pavements. All the above-named areas were within walking distance, with generic government or council houses, boasting additions and extensions. Most yards sported purpose-built shacks, dwarfed by the added rooms or double storeys, as we called them – a sure sign the owners carried heavier purses and wallets. The state of the house, yard and fences also gave an idea of the occupants, but anything appeared better than the shack I lived in.

Each area had a church or two and a primary school to share the community load. We were all in the same boat, yet kids took pleasure in belittling others from another area. The slight differences in our accents, dialect and physical traits, accounted for many a scuffle among kids along the dusty roads, pavements and pathways. English-speaking kids regarded themselves as more important than their Afrikaans counterparts, but we all found a common ground to eke out a daily living – borrowing, lending, sharing alike. We all knew our place in the community and home, despite all that was said and done. For us at the time, it was a silent struggle, unsure why we lived the way we did.

Across the vast forest lay unseen homes, gardens, churches, and schools of the rich or better off, they said. Buffalo Flats remained a mystery to me for about six years, the sun glinting off shiny rooftops, moving cars and the sole bus trekking down to us.

I never understood why the bus began its journey picking up rich people, leaving few or no seats for the poorer citizens. A graveyard for the coloured community was in an extension of Buffalo Flats, ironically called Ghost Town, an obvious nickname. I never had a reason to go there, not that I had funds and for many years, I wondered how the rich coloureds lived. Most households scrimped, saved, borrowed or begged, and ours was no different. It was fine accepting handouts to replenish and refurbish. Industrious shack owners sold anything to hungry, thirsty pedestrians, workers and school kids. From sweets, juices, homemade ice-lollies to ginger beer, fizzy drinks, nuts and toffee apples. Bokdrolle or goat droppings, a direct translation, were a treat for many kids. The small rounded brown sweet had the perfect crude crunchy chocolate taste for a poor scruffy barefoot kid.

Our favourite childhood treats were homemade toffee apples, ice-lollies and assorted bags of nuts or bits and pieces of crushed chocolate. Sweets from local shops paled in comparison to the real chocolate taste, and any kid who held a packet was targeted for some spoils. Snatch and grabs happened, or we circled, pleading, begging, noting any past favours or promising new ones. Anything to get some as harried kids ducked out of sight to eat in peace. We hated a kid who gloated without sharing, which was never a virtue among the poor. There was never a need to question how and why bits of dirt, stone and plastic were mixed with the sweets. We spat out or rinsed and swallowed. It made everything more exciting. Let the poor eat sweets, not cake.

The next sweet craze was a sheet of sweet gelatin, resembling bubble wrap. Washing off the dirt and grit, once again not questioning, we devoured everything. Sticking the gelatin into a palm of one hand and kneading it into a paste, we licked at it all day, to everyone's annoyance. Bullies cornered kids and shoved the sweet palm into the sand. Our angry parents warned us never to buy the dirty sweets or drinks since they came from the tip and were dirty.

"Tip, what is that?" we asked. We learned that shack dwelling sweet vendors visited the local dumping site or tip to scavenge through piles and piles of rubbish from factories and who knows where. Broken items were fixed, sold or reused. If it was edible, they repacked and sold them to poor hungry naïve school kids. The mangled chocolate bits and sweets came from a local sweet factory, Wilson Rowntree or Wilson's. So, our bits came from a proper sweet factory, big deal. We knew people working there and never stopped eating or drinking goodies bought from the shacks. What did adults know!

When money was tight, we decided to find this elusive tip with its treasure trove and set the record straight. After trekking via the forest, with arms, legs and faces itching, scratched and bitten, we found our beloved crushed, dirty treats and juices. That I live to tell this tale is an amazing miracle is all I would say. Weaning ourselves off those filthy sweets and recycled juices was the toughest part. Knowing that rats, rabid dogs, cats and scavenging humans fought over the same loot was enough to scar one for life. Despite a short interval of childish transgressions and stubbornness, we grew and thrived, stayed fit and healthy. Those mandatory measles, mumps and chickenpox got us isolated, covered in the vile smelling Calamine Lotion, itching while trying not to scratch. Parents sat us out in the sun to kill the germs and heal sores while friends teased us for being rabid. What came around, went around.

Missing school because of scabies, rabies or whatever, was not a bad thing, even if it meant staying indoors for most of the time. We used each other's badness and illness, madness, sadness or sometimes happiness as fodder for entertainment. Victims joined bullies, laughing in unison, feeding the audience and masses. I held my head high and looked down at times, getting on with life as society expected me to. As an adolescent, I had my fair share of mishaps before I became a teenager. A fall from a wall, a scar on my forehead and right wrist, running into two bicycles. Just to prove I was faster, I took another fall during an attempt at being a soccer player and sprained an ankle. Unable to step on my right foot, I came home on crutches. Hobbling, self-conscious, feeling quite useless, I vowed never to repeat this again. Out of circulation, I missed my suitors but not the bullies.

When I did venture out, they called me 'Hop along Cassidy' as I shuffled along on my crutches. Mr Cassidy was this fictional, rough talking, dangerous and rude storybook cowboy created in the early 1900's. We teased anyone with a walking disability, limp or crippled leg as the very man himself. Bittersweet irony.

Living in the small shack was very soul-destroying, even if I could not describe how I felt at the time. No one knew I shared a bed with my father, and I kept my home life a top secret from school friends and classmates. Surrounded by people living in similar conditions, our situation was not unique, yet I felt it was not normal even if it was the standard for many households. I had no idea if friends shared a bed with any parent. I had no idea what the norm was. At least I knew what a birthday meant. One got taller, older, and maybe cuter. One might have a party, but in our shack, the special day was nothing to make any fuss or fanfare about.

One went along telling people it was one's birthday, hoping a gift might surface and a kind word, a wave, a smile and perhaps promises of a gift in the future. Your birthday outfit had been paid off over a few months, only to double up as Sunday church wear. Sometimes a limp happy birthday song from your sleepy family, or none. There was that awkward kiss and hug, or a tap on the head and maybe some spare coins stuffed into your hand, and off you went. There was never a card, no cake and candles or any friends singing Happy Birthday to you. Nothing special was attached to a birthday for as long as I can recall, I have never had a birthday party held in my honour. As I write, I am turning fifty years old, and I am having a cake with fifty candles for me to huff and puff over.

Chapter 28: life was a beach among friends and races

Christmas and New Year's celebrations made up for all those unfilled birthday parties as parents, friends, neighbours, and relatives made up for the lack of luxuries over the year. The buildup to a new year was the same, homes got repainted, refurnished, and redecorated while we fretted over those new outfits waiting to be collected from shop shelves, dusty and usually out of fashion. My shiny three-piece suit got replaced by my spanking new shorts and sweater, no long pants or shirts for me. Kids minced, posed and pranced around, exchanging compliments or mocking other kids over their choice of outfit, generally chosen by insistent parents. Outfits were bought for longevity and less out of fashion sense. They were new, and that was all that mattered to us.

Sunday school and church service on Christmas Day took ages, kids fidgeted, and our parents let us race home to change. Kids and adults let their hair down as we counted the days until a new year's celebration. The party season had started, with the adults running the show while kids played watchdog and keeper at a price. Those able to afford holidays away from the shacks were waved off without a spot of envy or jealousy, of course. It was the season for great weather, goodwill, greedy kids and guarded parents. Because of the close living quarters, there was no avoiding the festive spirit preparation nor its repercussions. The good, bad and ugly was shared along with a lot of food, jelly, fruit salads and sweets, until parents put a stop to it.

Tomorrow was another day, they said. After one tomorrow too many, the eagerly anticipated New Year's celebrations were a joyous and stressful time for many. Everyone, or most people, had to get to the seaside, to end one year and begin another. We begged, rented and pimped, determined to go to the sea in the new year, no matter what. The coastal area designated for the non-whites in my city was quite far, but scorching sun and heat, heavy downpours or strong winds were no deterrent. No year was complete without a trip to eat, drink and be merry at Cove Rock or Leaches Bay.

I never really understood any reasoning for our long journey to these distant beaches, every coloured or mixed-race person coexisting happily together on this day. With no whites and a handful of blacks or Africans in sight, people descended onto the beaches for a day or two away from the drudgery of shack and home life. The extent and understanding of our social and cultural division was some years away, and I was blissfully unaware that my country had not created an equal platform for all its inhabitants.

Getting back to our annual festive party preparations, the cavalcade of cars crept at snail's pace, bumper to bumper, loud music blaring from speakers lined roads en-route to the beach. We passed frustrated drivers and campers helping with fallen goods, flat types, jump-starting or pushing cars, which were just about roadworthy. Excited semi-drunk drivers honked horns at passing traffic while their boozy passengers sang along to the music. Vans, cars or trucks crammed with food, utensils, drinks, chairs, tents or umbrellas, blankets, toys, cheap swimming costumes and the all-important crates and boxes of alcohol. Since the beaches were isolated, we packed for the long haul. Extra trips wasted time and petrol was costly. Those opting for a quieter day at home were going to wish they had not. The madness and mayhem ensued over the best camping spot or trying to secure the same one as the previous year. Friends became enemies over the best braai or barbecue areas or failing to reserve a spot for late arrivals. A brawl would erupt as tempers and high alcohol levels inflamed the disharmony, if only for a few minutes as we unpacked for the festivities to get underway. After unpacking, the friendship revival, mood lifting, and motivation would be unleashed. The coloured or 'bruin-ous' (brown people) had arrived.

Leaches Bay and Cove Rock were not ideal beaches for swimming, they said, but then I hardly knew any coloured person who could swim for that matter. My early visits to the beach around the farm or in Durban saw us stick to the breakwater and frolic in the surf. Big waves scared us and, warned of the undertow, we always played it safe. A semi-drunk adult enjoying a festive holiday out in the sun was another story altogether.

Cove Rock is one of South Africa's remarkable sandstone formations, and a place for breeding seabirds and whale watching, but for a coloured kid or adult, it was simply a beach for fun and games – happy to splash in the salty seawater because a full year would pass before we repeated the process. Settled campers gloated at the newcomers who bickered over camping spots; parents unpacked and screamed at the kids to stay close and not race to the enticing seawater and sandy beach. Excited voices echoed in the air, and loud music from different speakers sounded along the once-quiet stretch of beach.

The smell of food and salads wafted in the breeze. Semi-drunk men stoked or started fires to grill the many kilograms of raw meat, which was marinated and previously spiced. Tempers flared over forgotten or misplaced items.

No New Year's Day table or feast was complete without the huge ripe round watermelons, a summer fruit of all coloured households, a supply of cooked mealies, or corn on the cob, coming a close second. If forgotten, an opportunistic camper usually sold these items and more around the beach or we borrowed, loaned, and begged during this season of goodwill. We all wanted to relax, watch and enjoy the scenery and shenanigans.

Whichever beach you went to, the set up was almost identical regarding drinking, eating and socializing. Kids ate anything, and everything offered or pilfered, while the adults chose liquid refreshments instead. Warned not to swim with a full stomach, or wander too far, we pushed the boundaries, setting off in groups to explore old and new haunts. Loud voices and music grew faint as we enjoyed the fresh sea air. We dared each other to be brave and step as far into the sea as possible, only for someone to scream "Shark!" and laugh as we panicked to race back out. A group of wet happy kids returned for another helping of food and non-adult drinks.

Semi-drunk adults around the camping sites provided enough entertainment as we recharged our little batteries. Unimpressed wives and girlfriends watched the antics of their drunken partners and their tendency to test the tides, only to flail about in the surf and be rescued. Leaving the adults to their antics, we raced up and down sand dunes until we hurt, or the heat and sun drove us into hiding. My fun was always short-lived when other kids entered our space. Naturally, my social claim for kissing or being kissed by other boys was hardly a secret, and strangers were given a rapid update, adding to the bully count. And so, the hurtful verbal battering began as hands grabbed at me, while friends did their best to take my side. Nothing was going to stop the words cutting deeper, further denting my social confidence. Despite the brightness, I felt desolate. No one expected me to have fun without attempting to lower my self-esteem.

Racing away to hide, fully aware that they would follow, it was easier facing it alone than having my friends witness my public discrediting and shame. Once found, I let them do as they pleased. Pinning me to the ground, boys took turns in kissing me, not caring if I hurt or was marked. Assuming they were humiliating me, there was no outward sign of the happiness I felt. They used me without my permission, I gave little resistance, and I used the internal euphoria to cushion the emotional agony. Watching them walk away, cheerful and happy, I got up, dusted myself down before a walk back to join the others. I would attribute red flushed face and cheeks to the heat. I felt eyes on me, heard the whispers or loud derogatory remarks, yet remained stone-faced and steely-eyed. Only I felt the delicious tingling of my face, lips and skin.

Back at the camping sites, different music beats and sounds clashed, voices sounded a bit more animated and louder, plastic containers with ice housed the alcohol while the watchful owner kept a beady eye on who drank too much. We waited about and listened as they cheerfully recapped antics from yesteryear amid screams of laughter.

Mellowed and relaxed, we forgot about the shacks, the day to day grind, and the bid to make ends meet. I kept my distance from the drunk older boys and men who tried to get me alone with some lame excuse. Refusing to look rude or impolite to my elders, I left with them, only to run and safely sit among the adults. Sometimes I was not so lucky, as I begged them not to mark my skin. The unspoken request to be quiet and silent hung in the air. My presence seemed to bring out the worst in some people, who took pleasure in physically using a younger boy and letting him deal and cope with the emotional aftermath.

After the day's activities had been expended and enjoyed, with some people fortunate to be staying an extra day or two, the rest had to make their way back home. Starting the new year with a suntan or sunburnt skin made it exciting or uncomfortable and painful. Happy in our summer glow or irritated with the peeling skin, we would gladly repeat the whole day all over again, but sadly we had to wait for one full year.

Gossiping or retelling our seaside antics for days and weeks, we imprinted good and bad memories in our heads and hearts. Sadly, most people never owned cameras for a picture trail of these wonderful festive jaunts at the seaside. A blessing perhaps, to the party animals and their tomfoolery. while others may have cherished still images of a fun-filled and carefree time spent among the trees, dunes and sand on Leaches Bay or Cove Rock Beach.

Chapter 29: the eighties and the budding adolescent

As the seventies ended, I still lived in a tiny wooden shack while the bullies held me to ransom at every corner, but my many little boyfriends helped soothe most of the misery and loneliness. The worst part was having no one to talk to about what I was going through, or my unacceptable social attraction to other boys. Motivated with a personal obligation to impress friends and teachers with good grades, I studied hard and used my textbooks as an anti-social tool. The final year of primary school arrived and after all was said and written, I had joined the top ten bright pupils in class and of the school. My star shone brightly, though I was still shy, insecure and uncomfortable being on the receiving end of compliments and kind words. No one knew I spent hours with a candle or lamp, reading and studying in the outside toilet or behind the shack, when my mother nagged and complained about me wasting candles and paraffin. My parents and siblings may have seen a quiet obedient child; my peers knew me as a sissy and bullied kid with the emotional psyche of a girl. The Georgie at school was a different boy to the one they called David at home.

While I was engrossed in my scholastic pursuits, my sister left school, joining others in the job queues. Leaving school meant an immediate path to a workplace, since parents were in no mood to support an idle child. Their nagging alone drove one in search of a job, even if it meant loitering around corner stores, hoping and waiting for any work opportunity. With few options in our tiny seaside town, most young people were hired as tellers or cashiers, factory workers, and shop assistants by word of mouth. Relatives or friends jostled their nearest and dearest to the front of the job queue. My older sister got her first job at a clothing factory after someone put in a good word for her. That she was a very pretty girl might have helped too. Da Gama was a South African textile factory, and together with Wilson's Rowntree, the sweet confectioners, and Mercedes-Benz, the car manufacturer, they provided jobs to many local and migrant travellers. Despite being a fair distance from home, with early morning starts and multiple trips, my sister held up, and her small brown envelope filled with a pitiful salary added extra food on the table and clothes on our back.

Her younger brother was no slouch either. Frank sailed into high school even though we never saw him study around the place. He occasionally returned home with stacks of magazines, picture storybooks, comics and newspapers. Assuming local shops got rid of old stock, no one questioned him, excited for the written and visual diversion in the shack when days were dark, wet and miserable. We traded old or new books, keen and eagerly awaiting a to be continued copy.

Re-enacting stories and poses from a homegrown comic book called Tessa, the female undercover cop prancing around in swimwear, was my personal favourite. There was Kid Colt, the cowboy, published by Marvel, and comics we got to love, such as Ritchie Rich, Sad Sack, Little Lotta, Hot Stuff and Casper. And let us not forget Archie, Betty and Veronica or Jughead. The memories are engraved and endless. Die Swart Luiperd, The Black Panther, and Eerste Liefde, First Love, as well as other locally produced comics empowered us to become fictional characters. Behind closed doors and out of sight, no one saw me pose like Tessa, minus the swimsuit. Neither did they know I rolled my threadbare underpants until it resembled a bikini bottom for added effect. I was almost an obsessed storybook poser myself.

Every so often, Frank dropped money on the table, offering some inaudible reason for his financial reward. Welcoming the money, one got an impression it was payment for something about to go down. A letter arrived questioning whether Frank would return to school after his suspension. Well, that was a surprise, since my brother dressed and left for school every day. When and why was he suspended? Frank had been rude and disrespectful in class, prompting his suspension. It was rumoured he slapped a teacher, which we found hard to believe. My brother was so quiet and sedate, an image of him being aggressive was just too unbelievable. Thus, ended his schooling career, which was so sad since he was so clever. Frank was a delivery boy for a newspaper distributor in the area, leaving me the sole scholar in the shack.

Our white government gave a small monthly grant to unemployed or disabled parents to clothe and feed families. When a child reached employable age, showing any signs they would falter or not finish school, everyone encouraged them to seek a job. A lack of good educational role models around the shacks only added to their assurances that money could be made from a young age. Finishing high school was an expectation no shack kid imagined, as some ignored whispers to find a job to give back to parents for raising, feeding, clothing and educating them. Thus far I had escaped scrutiny, and no one forced me to attend. It was my duty as a child since I had nothing to bring to the table.

Despite the two meagre pay packets and small monthly government disability grants, the Calverley home always seemed to need money for something. Being the child in the house, I was the debt and money collector. Dragging my feet, for once the bullying a welcome distraction, I knocked on the door, waiting for a response to enter or wait. They knew the reason for my presence and played out a pantomime, with me as the stooge. Waiting outside, I heard whispering, should they give all or some of it, or nothing at all. A suggestion that I return the next day was the usual feedback.

Debt collection was around dinnertime, the food smell making my tummy grumble as I heard them scrape spoons on enamel plates. I had never seen anyone use a knife and fork during a meal. Not invited indoors to wait and witness the meal table, I felt like a beggar, hating the fact I had to repeat the process a few days later. It was soul destroying, to say the least. It hurt returning empty-handed and seeing my heartbroken parents' hope deflate at the thought of not providing a plate of food for their kids.

Except we were not kids anymore. Two were working teenagers, and I was about lose my adolescent title. At thirteen, I still slept next to my dad, at the foot end of a single bed. There was no space, or money, for a larger one, and I was too tall to curl up into a tight ball. We battled for bed space, accounting for nine years of a disturbed sleeping pattern, but my discomfort was far from over. No one warned me changes were about to take place. Suddenly I began to sprout soft black hairs on my arms and legs, in my armpits and in my private area. Unhappy with this new development, I used a lighted candle, trying to burn them as we did to the dead plucked chickens before cooking. A strange smell and pain put a stop to that quite quickly. Telling no one of my act of self-mutilation, I let nature take its course. My boyhood period had come to a hairy end.

228

All the new prickly hairs took some getting used to, but it never deterred my suitors at all. Not every boy was blessed with manly thistles, which was a blessing or a curse. A newly sprouted boy preened and gloated, inviting others to peer down his pants to see the ball hairs, as the playground became a mass of testosterone driven boys. Any claims of ball hairs had to be seen to be believed. Kids were wrestled or pinned down while hands reached into shorts to expose, confirm or negate pubic hairs. Boys with a full crotch of hair were going to be men and not sissies, they mocked. This poor sissy had hair everywhere yet hardly felt, acted or behaved like a boy. How was crotch hair going to make a man out of me?

Our growing pains were only just beginning. It was nothing to be ashamed over, and even the high-spirited teasing and bullying were a welcoming distraction. Body hairs set in place, our voices boxes took over, playing tricks when least expected. A shrill falsetto or a sudden deep base had everyone in stitches. One had no control over vocal chords, and I fought those deep tones because I wanted to sound like a girl.

Departure from boyhood was a mixture of pain and pleasure. Waking up and feeling a hard stub under my nipples was another mystery. They were prominent, sensitive and tender to touch. My suitors took much interest in mine rather than their own, and for the first time we noticed something different. When they rubbed my nipples, I had a strange if not tingling sensation in my chest and crotch. Unsure of this new development, it sent many more boys in my direction. I was not sure if they experienced the same thing as I did. Parading my budding bosom with pride,

I bounced around, insisting I deserved a bra for my sissy boobs.

Like the crotch hairs, nipple stubs were another source of teasing and bullying. Mini breasts lingered if one hated them, but not before wreaking embarrassment or havoc on their owner. There were no escaping these short sudden and strange changes. It was something I dealt with on my own. Predictable attention from boys cemented my feelings and I milked everything for its worth, no not my nipples as they flattened and left me looking like my usual boyish self.

I battled many feelings that were part of my personal, physical, and mental growth at this time, and perhaps still struggle with them as I write this book. Whether my parents and siblings noted my gradual shifting from adolescence, no one mentioned anything. Of course, my sister and brother suffered the same changes, yet I do not recall fanfare or fuss about it. My brother or father certainly never educated me about anything, so I used friends and bullies to provide light relief and backyard preparation in sharing the journey into juvenile maturation.

However, I could not stop rough hands or harsh words hurled my way. That feeling of taking two steps forward and ten backwards never left me. Accepted one minute, and suddenly I got isolated and terrorized for what I was or what they perceived me to be. The number of suitors decreased as they fought physical changes and hormones while common sense or social awareness prevailed in some. A real boy had no right kissing another boy, no matter how much of a sissy he was. We had reached a plateau when it was safe to say that a boy had to be kissing a girl and I had no intention of doing that and told no one. Neither did I mention the fact I had reached the age of puberty whereby I could father a child.

Secretly the sissy had become a man. Hiding the fact was another kettle of fish. Sleep peppered with dreams, weird sensations and waking to an unfamiliar wetness, yet not a smell of urine. A dry bed added to the riddle until playground operatives solved the conundrum, as you learned that your wet dreams and nightly emissions were normal and a sign of turning the ultimate page into manhood. However, it also had a very public way of letting others onto your secret.

My school attendance record was perfect, unless bad weather or illness kept me away. Getting out of the shack was the better option and running to Sharon's house for most of the day was the other. My classmates and I had one last examination to get through before a single year of junior high, and another four-year educational stretch, to reach a goal our parents, siblings or relatives had not achieved or for some reason had been denied. Not feeling any pressure, my main aim was to impress friends and teachers. A bully suggested that being studious was a typical sissy trait. Staying focused was hard, but I put the imposed isolation and solitude to good use. There was a quiet composure no one could shake, assured they knew it, provoking them even further.

I truly studied under the cover of darkness, spending most of the daytime revising and wondered why my classmates could not do the same. They had electricity and enough space, yet most crammed and stressed until the last minute. It was the nerdiest school kid who did homework and studied on time. About five years had passed, Durban had become a distant memory, old friends and tormentors, faces and names blurred in with the new ones. The chances of seeing or meeting them again grew slimmer and I often wandered if they missed or thought about me.

Word trickled our way that the gangs and drug dealers had reduced the place to a rough and scary habitat, nothing like the happy place we found and cultivated. Many had no option but to stay and watch the unsavoury activities escalate and consume the young men of the area. Relieved, yet still unsure why we had left the rainbow chicken houses, I thanked my lucky stars but felt sad for those who still suffered those nightly raids and the drunken fights as friends became enemies, trying to maim and damage each other while under the influence of drugs and alcohol. Maybe a vigilant guardian angel had spread his wings over my parents, siblings and me.

Chapter 30: achieving that primary objective

The time to leave primary school had arrived, but one last examination was yet to be conquered. Nervous and excited about moving to a new school, I was not going to be left behind. All I wanted was a good pass mark. I never doubted myself, despite having problems with some of my schoolwork. Especially woodwork, as a practical subject, which I hated with a passion. All my fingers turned into thumbs and struggled with the rulers, clamps, compasses and protractors, assuring everyone I was not the budding builder, boilermaker or candlestick maker. Teased and told to join the girls in needlework, the theoretical part of woodwork class was a breeze. I merely regurgitated the textbook. I could not draw lines, make curves or shapes for the life of me. It was odd.

The nights spent squinting in the near darkness came to an end. Taking home my last report of my primary school years, I passed with flying colours. My lowest mark was for woodwork, as expected, but the fifty percent pass mark for theory was enough. Many of my classmates had passed, but we would be separated from those moving to a high school in the Indian area or community. Good grades or not, it was one step closer to being employable, a fine achievement and making our parents proud. Head held high, I watched as my poor parents scrounged around for a brand-new uniform during my last school holidays as a primary school sissy boy.

They had to procure long grey pants to cover my thin hairy legs, a new green jersey, a green and white striped tie, and an expensive green blazer. Our faded white shirts were not going anywhere. Secondhand gear was the order of the day and a green school blazer a dream for a kid from the poor side of town.

It was never going to materialize. Most of the educational paraphernalia we had to provide or pay a fee for – despite the meagre funds in most households, or the lack of funds entirely. Hating my shiny long suit pants, I dreaded wearing long school trousers. It was fun wearing shorts to school and around the house, but for the next five years I had to wear long pants for most of the day. How would I cope?

If we could afford the dark green track pants and top with a single white stripe down the side of the legs and arms, it would be a bonus. As we frolicked in the sea and sand to celebrate the end of 1980, our skin tanned or peeling, we got back to reality and a set of new and old school gear ready to be worn. Dressed up neatly, we proudly made our way towards the new school, a long walk away in the hot boiling sun – a full forty-five minutes or more, to be exact.

Along the way, there were some bare legs in short grey pants, and I was one of those people. I felt uncomfortable in my new shoes and uniform. As we passed along, people waved and shouted words of encouragement and congratulations for getting this far. Dressed in some semblance of a junior high school uniform, we must have looked presentable, if not scared and unsure of the year ahead. The lack of funds would make this journey somewhat arduous, especially during strong winds, heavy downpours, high humidity and the searing sun. Warned that our next adventure was no child's play, we had to be responsible and it was time to grow up. We also had to prove they had done a good job and prepared us for the next few academic years. Pefferville Primary and the teachers had a reputation to uphold, like every other primary school in the area whose pupils were to join us in junior high school.

Walking towards the school situated in North End, a suburb close to the city, my new pair of black shiny shoes, Hush Puppies, squeaked and pinched with each step. We all watched, eyed and assessed each other as kids from neighbouring schools joined the long line of adolescents and teenagers. Dressed to blend in with the crowd, everyone knew who I was, and they teased, and name called as if it was the most accepted thing in the world. Fixated on getting to the gate without being pulled and touched, I took no notice of our privileged classmates staring at us from passing cars, escorted to the school while we trudged up the final incline. Dropped a few feet from the gate, fresh, clean and unruffled, they may have looked upon us with pity while we trekked along the road, sweaty and uncomfortable before we reached the gate. Knowing we faced a full year ahead, we reached an imposing brick building and entered the gates as brand-new scholars of St Johns Road Primary School.

Situated at a busy four-way intersection, close to the sweet factory, Wilson's, the loud and noisy traffic sounds were going to be distracting. Herded down a sandy tree-lined slope towards the back of the school, we huddled together for our very first assembly as junior high school kids. Proud, expectant yet anxious about this new chapter in our lives, the principal and his staff welcomed us to the entering class of 1981.

A shy slim adolescent with black curly hair and a voice with a mind of its own, I was grouped with many of my old friends into Class O, one of three English classes. Over the next year, teachers would prepare us for a high school career while we had to deal and cope with our raging hormones. There was nothing we could do but allow our bodies to be moulded and modified into mini adult ones. My parents and friends watched me transform and morph from one shy adolescent to a scrawny, spotty and very insecure teenager over the next five years.

Chapter 31: st john's road primary school shenanigans

Our new school's motto was Per ardua ad astra, translating into Through adversity to the stars or Through struggle to the stars. One of the oldest co-educational schools in the area, it had remained a fixture during a time when non-white people were evicted and relocated, and buildings demolished by the white government of South Africa. We did not have much knowledge about the time mentioned above or why we were given the bare basics, but they expected us to reach for the stars. We accepted the challenge with a youthful passion, hoping to impress old and new teachers. Punctuality, good manners, neatness and being a good role model for the schools were important. We were not to act like naughty kids, they said, except we were still children.

The new teachers wasted no time in dishing out punishment over things we took for granted in primary school. Tardiness, missing lessons, failing tests, late homework or missed assignments were huge transgressions. A stern verbal warning, embarrassing to say the least, and a wooden ruler or cane were used with good effect. The bruised or burning backside or hand, and a stinging ego, only worked for short periods though. It took a lot to keep us in line, and some teachers targeted a certain section of kids when dishing out punishment and lashes, the severity and number of lashes depending on a lot of things. Excuses, genuine or fake, were often ignored or deemed irrelevant, once again to a portion of kids. We did take note, grumbling and mumbling under the pain and injustice, fighting the urge to rub hands or buttocks, or shove a stinging hand under an armpit or between your thighs because crying in public was not an option.

Detention after school was the worst punishment. They were being cruel but kind, yet we viewed it differently. Friends gleefully ran out and home, as the indifferent teacher sat doing his homework and we grumbled and pleaded, but to no avail. The kids living on the poor side of town had reasons to fear as they straggled home alone. Sometimes we all suffered because of one person's mistake or naughtiness.

Our trips to school were nothing short of eventful. I spoke about the bad weather, our paltry bus service, and those dubious taxi drivers, but then there was the odd good Samaritan. No free rides were ignored, but fights broke out over who deserved the lift as drivers watched us push, charge and shove for a seating space, often driving off in disgust or amusement. We took risks by scaling fences and cutting through yards, the angry owner setting dogs after us as we trampled flower gardens and dashed into open doors to escape the frothing mongrel. Sudden weather changes, irate yard owners, and a spitting canine were the least of our worries along the dusty and dirt lined roads.

We passed an area known as Durban Flats, notorious for its share of young boys and men looking to cause trouble. As a matter of fact, every area had an aimless bunch of loiterers on street and shop corners, terrorizing people going about their daily duties. Not all were bad, though we feared them anyway. Trying to appear cool and relaxed, one gave little or no eye contact as we walked along in a group or alone. We were no match for them either way, so it was very important and wise to avoid detention after school.

Durban Flats had no actual flats, but low roofed houses built close together and some makeshift shacks knocked up next to them. Despite individual doors, the place looked like one large shack from the main road. Many years later, when I found the courage to venture further afield, I found a residential area no different to our own. Except the thugs near or around us never relieved us of our bus and taxi fares, lunches, schoolbooks or items of clothing for a laugh. Bread, milk, sugar, cigarettes were confiscated too, as angry parents refused to imagine or believe one was robbed in broad daylight. For the next year and another four, if we passed into high school, hell and harassment awaited us, but we stayed focused on the main prize, along with other issues at school.

St John's Road primary accommodated junior high school coloured and Indian kids in the area. A motley crew of poor, middle class, and rich pupils circled and watched one another, misconceptions and attitudes creating a playful bullying arena before settling into a comfortable camaraderie and friendships. Our varying dialects, accents and the obvious social divide, coupled with our personal mannerisms and behaviours, were a great source of fun and entertainment at the start. There were the bright kids, the class clowns, the bookworms, those annoying socially confident kids picking on the shy and quiet scholar, and every other character in between. We had a full year to make some friends or asses each other, but the war between rich and poor, the different groups of Afrikaans against English speaking pupils, hung over our heads. The local kids had each other and friends for support while others joined the public and private feud.

A bunch of kids known as the hostelites came from further afield to attend schools in our area. These boarding school dwellers often had a rough time, shunned, bullied or mistreated by the local pupils. I knew what being the new kid on the block felt like. It was not very nice, and after five years or so, I was still ostracized for being wired a bit differently. There was no one else like me, or perhaps there was, and I was too busy fighting my own battles to notice, so I watched them bully kids from another town or city. Knowing they had left friends and family behind, kind words and friendly faces were what they needed the most. Most were from neighbouring towns while some did cross state lines at the time, arriving from the Transkei, my dad's birthplace.

Another short history lessons. The Transkei and Ciskei were two areas created for the local South African black people by the white apartheid government. There were ten such "homelands" in total scattered around the country and its borders. Transkei got its "independence" in 1976, maintaining a strict border for travellers and visitors alike. Our junior high school class was an ethnic bag of kids with varying skin tones, hair threads, eye colour and dialects, and yet we shared a common bond. Everyone was a coloured, thanks to our ancestors or grandparents who created our parents, and so the white government of the country punished us for that reason. At this point, the full extent of the sanctions and penalties were the furthest from our little minds. We had no reason to second guess the state of our welfare, other than to make the most of it.

Our teachers were no different to any we had had before. There were the excellent, good and bad or indifferent ones, but mostly they commanded our attention and expected a load of respect always. Not all kids were geared to behave or revere authority. The raging teenage hormones could be blamed here, with a brazen few applying their own dose of histrionics to garner some clout around the school. Those who promised to be well-behaved and not disgrace our former teachers sat back in awe and fascination. It was going to be an interesting year, so we settled down to make the most of it. Looking around the classes, we had a lot to learn about social etiquette and graces.

It did not help that the school stood near a four-way stop, so the constant sounds of noisy traffic interfered with and disrupted classes. Over time, teachers and pupils adopted a comfortable pattern as we got to know, understand, love and dislike each other. The new school, like our primary one, had a very relaxed view when it came to sport, arts and outdoor activity classes.

Like before, physical education depended on the weather, available space and the mood of the teacher. There was a steep sandy incline, muddy when it rained, which led to a large uneven grassy plain and a tarmac square behind the school. The dress code also derived from the effort and enthusiasm of the pupils and the lack of money. The heat, sun or rain added to that too. Lack of equipment was standard if not expected, so with little motivation and encouragement, the period ended up being a free-for-all. We fell short on so many levels, and with few benchmarks for that matter, we remained dead and clueless as to how much the white government withheld, delayed and denied our full potential and robbed the community of many a great sportsman or -woman.

Wait a second, perhaps we could tease and taunt them with a little taste of something, they might have discussed among themselves. Approaching the playground one day, I noticed a strange contraption on the grass. Before us stood a square leather-covered box with two steel handlebars and wooden four legs, resembling a horse with no head or tail. The teacher proudly announced we could hop, skip, jump or somersault over it and when gripping the handles, we could swing our bodies in a circle, do a handstand before alighting. Only for the agile and flexible, of course. A lame display with some lack or little confidence, we watched and gingerly circled the high leather box. At the age of thirteen, some fourteen, it was our very first personal introduction to the sturdy pommel horse used in artistic gymnastics.

Secondly, I had no idea there was an artistic side to gymnastics, boxed into the idea it was only about cartwheels, handstands and back flips on a thick plastic mat. This poor kid had a lot to learn, but right now, I was happy to be a dainty spectator as I watched the boys get on with it. Or try to at best.

The pommel horse was designed as an artificial horse for soldiers to learn how to get on and off a horse during combat and war. One needed muscle and technique, and my peers and I lacked one or the other, so after a few minutes on the fake horse, it did turn out to be a total disaster. We teased each other over weak attempts as we fell and fumbled until we resorted to a sporting activity we knew or preferred. After its single and auspicious appearance, our leather-wrapped pommel horse disappeared, never to grace the grassy plains of St John's Primary again. Alas, they had no other gadgets or toys waiting in the wings for the rest of the year, so it was safe to say that never was a gymnast going to come from our school or community.

Sporting equipment, facilities and decent proper coaching were not the only things our schools or classes lacked. A bigger void existed when it came to art class. Very little, if anything, artistic was ever performed or taught. It was basically a free period, but sometimes we took it upon ourselves or tried to sing, draw, or sketch, and have a stint painting or playing with clay, dry or wet. Generally, things turned dirty and we misbehaved, mocked and belittled those who tried their hand at something. Kids were hesitant, as no one wanted to be a laughing stock, so there was almost zero nurturing or cultivating of our artistic temperaments, whether we had it on our bones or not.

There was little or no speech or drama, dance, written, visual or mental art infusion for the coloured learner. Well, let me clarify, at least a poor coloured pupil. Little did we know our white counterparts were trained to dance, sing, mime, act and pirouette while being versed in all things cultural, sporty and artistic. They had sets of pummel wooden horses, they swung or jumped from bars, ropes and pulleys, and even got swimming and diving lessons. I had never been in a proper swimming pool.

Since we knew nothing about their wonderful life at school, there was no jealousy or envy. We had so little, and at no time did I think of myself as underprivileged. It was around me, we were all in the same boat, and we were poor and coloured. That was the extent of my understanding. Naturally, our parents mumbled and grumbled about things, but we never took notice of them. Everyone around us seemed ignorant, unconcerned, or misinformed about our lot in life, and we just lived through it from day to day.

I remained close to Irwin and Sharon, and luckily, we were in the same class. It did not take long for new boys to enter the picture, and there were the friendly and jocular sort, many of whom I encouraged and entertained. The outside bullies were part of my daily life, and there was nothing I could do except ignore them as much as I could. I was under constant, if not persistent, scrutiny. My private misery had been coated with protective layers over the years to prevent any public or emotional breakdown.

We shared classes, desks, and teachers, yet there was an invisible line separating us in terms of where and how we lived, dressed, spoke and behaved. Every class had some bright, studious, lazy, annoying and disruptive kid, as well those handsome and pretty ones. Brash, loud, confident and obnoxious kids scared me to death, aware they chose the quiet, shy and meek to tease or use as bait to entertain. Some of our teachers were young, handsome and pretty, which made classes somewhat easier, even if the subject was boring. We wanted to impress, and our hormones added an extra bit of excitement when least expected. I told no one how much I liked some boys in and around school, how I felt about my male teachers and had no one to share my pain when they shared their distaste for someone like me.

Not everyone fell for my sissy boy act, and there was one teacher. I hated his subject even more. Practically I was doomed but made up for it in theory. Those forty-five minutes were sheer hell and torture as we struggled being in the same room at once. The years of bullying had turned me into a hardened customer, so I took it on the chin and tried to stay out of his sight, praying the year would rush by. Some of the teachers were not good at teaching their own subjects, much less any other, so when a regular teacher was away, we had a free period, or some hapless replacement tried to control a very disruptive class.

There were those who knew how to cajole a teacher from a spur-of-the moment test and next-day assignments, but we were also quite aware they favoured the rich kids in class. Sounding more refined and posh, they were more confident

244

and self-assured in and out of class, something most of us lacked. Dressed in bright and full uniform, our pale faded second-hand versions were lacklustre in comparison. They were dropped a few feet from the school gate, fresh and clean, while we trekked along the road, sweaty and uncomfortable before we reached the gate. Never late, they were immune to most of the struggles we faced. Fearing and revering our teachers, these richer kids were at ease and almost too friendly with most of the teachers and school staff.

Once one looked past the residential codes, physical attributes, social airs and graces, the bunch of adolescents filled with raging hormones, got along despite some minor squabbles. Considering we might spend the next five years together, it was imperative we get on, tolerate and look out for one another. Our hazardous and jaunty trips brought us close, and we learned how to cope with the fearsome thugs and to face bullies. Educationally it was each man for himself, and we put all the other issues aside, knuckling down for a bit of hard graft and school work. The June and September examination results would determine those most likely to make it into high school the following year. Having to trek so far to school was a huge factor to make it through.

Chapter 32: dropping the I, made no difference

Thirteen, going on fourteen, I had grown taller yet stayed slim, probably from lack of good food and from all the running around. My arms, legs and chest were covered in short black hairs, and some of my suitors decided I was not quite a girl anymore. Shawn on the other hand kept me close and so did Daniel, my shy green-eyed friend. Boys near the shop and Ronald, alone or aided by sidekicks, tormented me whenever they fancied, while someone inevitably screamed, laughed, jeered, pointed or commented if I made an appearance. It was vital that everyone knew I was a sissy as I minced to and from class or school, trying to evoke a verbal and physical response from me. I never took the bait.

David to family and friends and Georgie to teachers and classmates, I looked aloof, calm and unaffected while I silently wept. I transitioned from childhood to adolescence and became a teenager with the help of some crude public and private education. My dear family played no role at all, nor did they prepare me for the myriad changes. It was down to my suitors and bullies. My brother and sister had come of age too, and it was a secret and silent affair. The confusing metamorphosis was not complete, and we had a lot to learn about our coloured and Pondo culture – our ancestral tribe – when it was time to become a fully-grown man.

Now, I was a scared schoolboy, hiding in class during breaks before overbearing and ruthless prefects who dragged me outside and watched the bullies descend. No amount of begging helped, because it added to their power trip as Irwin and I faced the packs of tormenting kids. Pressed up against the wall, we took it on the chin, Irwin flexing his nails to keep me from being hauled away and out of sight. As the other kids frolicked and ran about freely, we stood aside, wishing to join or be part of a game without any kid being derogatory or insulting.

My friend and I took each day as it came, and there was a boy who often came a bit too close for comfort. His wandering hands and teasing words and eyes made up for the misery during school hours. Tall and lanky, he resembled Andrew, my running partner. Accustomed to the playful teasing, it was a surprise when Clarence, a boy from the rich side of town, sat next to me before classes started. The school desks or bunks sat one or two kids at the time, great for those wishing to share a test paper or copy homework. The constant play of musical chairs during class was exciting, as kids avoided the class outcast and clown or deviant. Clarence was a good boy, sporty and friendly, so I never stopped or fought back when he teased, pinched or provoked me during a lesson. I had to pretend, giving suitably shocked expressions when he went too far. Keeping the straightest of faces when a hand is stroking its way down your back is not an easy job while listening to the lesson. Whispering silly nothings, his low voice set my face and cheeks on fire.

It had been some time since I noticed a strange sensation or feeling in my groin and it set me wriggling in my seat. Thanks to my crude educational team of boys, it seemed they knew how to unsettle me. Clarence's closeness, his whispering and touch made me skittish and excited at the same time. There was no point trying to fight nature. It was best surrendering to the glands of my growing body, and to the flirting, of course.

While I was enjoying his hand on my back, Clarence touched a sensitive spot, my body jerked, and I giggled. The teacher turned at the intrusion and asked me to share the joke, but I sat frozen, wondering if the others knew what we were up to. After an angry silence, I was told to stop acting like a girl and it was time for me to grow up. She advised me that they would call me George from this day forth. All this giggling and smiling and acting as if I was a girl had to stop. There would be no more Georgie.

That was how we came to the name change. But dropping the single letter made no difference. Boys continued to push me against the wall, they sat next to me, flirting, touching and pulling at my skin and clothes. I loved the attention and did my fair share of encouraging too. David to relatives and family members and now George to my school friends, the rest just called me a sissy. No wonder I was one confused little boy.

Despite artistic deprivation in our school, when a fundraising effort or concert, as we knew it, was being organized in the community, someone suggested we perform a play to add some spice to the programme. Experience taught us that the community concerts turned into one great fiasco, as cast and audience clashed on and off stage. This bunch of determined kids was not deterred as the excitement grew. Since I could not dance, sing, or act, I had no hopes of joining the cast. Besides I had little knowledge of all the things relating to musicals and stage plays. They were certainly not going to put a shy sissy in front of an audience. Since we never danced, sang or acted in class, except by being a fool or prankster in class, we wondered which lucky stars would grace the planks.

Surprisingly, there were some very talented kids around the place, and we watched the rehearsals in awe. The singing, dancing, fighting and acting had to be perfect. Kids at the bottom end of the acting chain were drafted to fill the stage as gangsters. This was a stretch considering that I was docile. My acting talents were going to be stretched to the hilt, but I found a way to hide in the crowd or right at the back and out of sight. Scared to mess up the proceedings, I secretly embraced the experience, delighted to add my own bit of extra volume to the cast. I did feel very important too. There was a special glow or pleasure in being part of a team of kids working towards a goal. Outsiders derided us in jealousy, but some complimented and encouraged us as the night of the concert inched towards us.

Parkside Hall was filled with friends, families, and of course, the usual gate- crashing villains. Loitering kids, adults and passing drunks were drawn to the bright lights, parked cars and milling crowds. They demanded free entry and meals, creating pandemonium and arguments before, during and after the event. Distractions, vocal or physical were part and parcel of the coloured community efforts to stage a peaceful gathering or concert, especially when a door fee was expected. The word "fundraising" was lost on them.

We were not going to be distracted as we sang, danced, acted, and fought across the stage with delight. I was happy to mime and pretend and did my best. We did a good job of it too. There was not a hint that we lacked or had no singing, acting, dancing, arts, drama lessons or training, and I thought that it was quite impressive. The joke was on me when I got informed that ballet and modern dance – not just ordinary dancing, acting and singing classes – were the norm for most of my classmates and other scholars from the better part of the community. I thought about my poor improvised yet enthusiastic dance sessions in the tiny wooden shack, burning to better my modern dancing skills, whatever they were.

The people missing from that night were of course my parents and siblings. I became adept at not telling them about my extracurricular shenanigans, leaving the shack and giving some lame excuse for my disappearance. Keeping my socially inept parents in the dark and away from friends and teachers, I wanted to save my own face, yet most parents I knew were no different to mine. So, what was my issue, if not to deprive the fundraising effort of ticket sales and my parents of a good night out?

What did my poor, uneducated parents know about musicals and stage plays anyway? Highlighting the question and justifying my shame in having Elizabeth and Archie as parents and a shack as a home. I was saving everyone from social embarrassment since my parents were quiet, shy and socially awkward like me. Huge, noisy crowds or people overwhelmed us, for different reasons naturally.

My mother usually spoke to strangers only when approached, hated drawing attention to herself, and sat quietly for hours, never sharing her thoughts or daydreams. We never asked, and it was not an uncomfortable silence, her infrequent conversations relating to simple day to day things. She seemed at peace with everything around her, in her own space. If it meant joining a group or being part of the public, she fussed over everything, making sure she only spent the required amount of time before going back to the privacy of a small clean shack. My dad watched people from the sidelines. Supporting his frame on a wooden walking stick, his quiet reassuring presence attracted people and before long, they would have lengthy conversations. My dad had this serene aura about him, as did my mother, despite their very different and opposing personality traits at home. There was nothing frantic or hurried about their demeanour away from the public or social eye. How these two met, courted, and married remains a perfect mystery to me.

Subconsciously, I was merely protecting them from finding out or hearing what other kids said or thought of me. Bullies thrived and grew in confidence when they had the chance to demean and belittle you in front of your friends or family. They always had to have one up on you, keeping you down and in your scared place. It was healthier to separate my school and home life for my own sanity, sustaining David, the good boy at home, while bolstering George, the shy sissy persona riddled with a heap of sexual, identity, social and personality issues.

Chapter 33: a fresh-faced boyish teenager, only in my dreams

Before we knew it, our year at St John's was coming to an end for those who worked and studied hard, while for some this was the breaking point. A passing grade meant the start of a high school career, while others might have to repeat the year or join long lines of job seekers. Cash-strapped parents mumbled over bus or taxi fares, or a fresh round of schooling essentials, sometimes delicately mentioning a job option and money to be earned. They coaxed relatives into applying extra pressure too. I knew I would pass, the next step inevitable, yet I felt very isolated and alone. Using my textbooks as an excuse and company, I felt like a pariah, aware I had to impress kids who barely liked, accepted or appreciated me. People often asked if there was an inner drive or personal aspiration to do good or be better, and my answer was a big, resounding No! Attending school and being a well-behaved child was the expectation, and while different childhood experiences sculptured a confused and insecure adolescent, there was still a lot of growing up to be done in my case.

Over the past six years, our tiny shack had had makeovers, yet it was never extended for its growing occupants, nor was there any talk of relocating. The wallpaper, linen, linoleum and curtains matched in colour, or what would people say? After staring at crappy wallpaper for most of my childhood, I developed a dislike to many things from my past, while it remains tough to release my inner demons.

People or shacks boasted many a self-made household or clothing item. Embroidered, knitted or crocheted multi-colored bed covers, jerseys and ponchos, which were big in the 70's and 80's, were a staple winter item for us. Some were made to order for sale as people sold anything and everything to make some extra cash. My mother sold cigarettes, the odd mixture of sweets, matches and other smaller items, but constant knocking on our door ended her small home industry after some time.

Some interesting information, as I gather thoughts: crochet is French, meaning small hook; embroidery comes from an ancient Chinese era and knitting from the English word knot. The earliest knitted cotton socks came from Egypt, where it was originally a male-only occupation. Ironically, I got called a sissy for trying my hand at knitting and crocheting with the girls.

On a serious note, there was no formal classification for what I had been through at the hands of Harvey, the boys and other kids. The nasty name calling overshadowed the playful teasing and games I got to play or join. Those playful mocking moments were accepted, if not part of our daily routine to fight the drudgery, poverty and hunger. Every child had its turn and depending on your status within the play group or setting, you dusted yourself off and moved on. It was just unfortunate that I was dissimilar to other boys and thus apparently deserved all the social, emotional and physical persecution. A bully and his actions have much more serious and damaging effects on their victim and prey. They had planted hurtful seeds of insecurity, low self-esteem and lack of confidence, activating the isolation and loneliness, all of which were kept watered daily. No one had any idea how much it would affect the social, emotional and psychological growth of the one being bullied. In my case, I had little concept of how I got through each day without falling apart.

Feeling like an intruder in my family shack, my daily suffering at the hands of bullies increased my discomfort around my parents and siblings. I observed them and slept a few feet away yet distanced myself and never got to know them. I fought many inner demons, keeping them tucked away and out of sight. We were five strangers bundled into a shack, bound by blood and left to get on with life.

My parents, siblings and I were almost insular in a way. Thinking back, there was not a lot of physical affection at home. We must have looked socially awkward as a family to outsiders. Since we never brought friends home and had few visitors to the shack, we were lonesome strangers to the outside world. Watching to imitate and learn, we played games, imagining a home life so different from the one we knew and lived through. The television provided us with new sets of ideas and fantasy, and we hoped never to make or repeat any mistakes. Parents made sure we knew the importance of keeping shame and disgrace away from the doorstep.

Privately ashamed of who and what I was, old enough to understand I was hated over it, I harboured no hatred, bitterness or anger towards my bullies or society at the time. I only wanted to be me, not fully understanding their dislike, issue or fascination with the sissy adolescent in their midst. I do not recall anyone asking about my feelings or why and how I became a sissy. Nobody offered much support, fearing they would be labelled or targeted too. Walking around, I felt that everyone saw right through me, while I remained wary, unsure and tense around boys and men in general.

There was a white farmer who drove around the area in a huge truck, stopping to chat with kids and adults along the way. I had no idea how or why he came around, but we hung onto the slow-moving vehicle at his encouragement. At first, we stared at him in awe, but he was so casual and friendly that kids jumped on the truck when he gave the invitation. He drove around the dusty streets with barefoot kids running alongside for the thrill. For some reason, I was happy to join those hanging onto the side, never getting into the front seat with him. He bought stuff from my dad's garden and then it was a matter of trying to coax me into the truck for a ride and carry out a plan he had in store. He may have seen me for what I was, but from my past experiences, I had an idea what was expected of me.

Raised not to be rude or disobey our elders, white, brown or otherwise, I fled as soon as the truck came into view, before my naïve father offered me as helper to load what he sold to the white stranger. He watched my every move, assured I was different and perhaps easy prey. He was not unlike the other men who pestered me from their yards or doorsteps, offering a gift of sorts if I stepped inside. Somehow, I stayed away and kept a suitable distance from the white farmer. His visits became less frequent, finally fading from our sight but not from my mind. I wondered about the kids who went along for the ride, and if the ride was purely an innocent gesture and nothing more.

Embracing my sexual confusion, I allowed, if not encouraged, male peers and boys to treat me as the emotionally charged girl I thought I was. To everyone else I was either a boy or girl, depending on the mood, social or private situation. Desperate and eager to please, I let them use, abuse and take advantage of me, giving everything, I had and not expecting much or anything in return. I wanted to be liked, loved and not hurt, but that was a tall order.

Seemingly I learned to reject and delay my personal gratification and happiness to please those around me, oblivious and unaware I laid a future pitted with many years of self-doubt and a solid foundation of inner turmoil. We still have a long way to go in this tale, so please stick around to find out how I fared. It would make me very happy indeed.

As a blossoming teenager, I knew right from wrong and much about every mixed bit in between. I was a miniature adult, developed enough to make kids and decisions, but that may be pushing it. Okay, my parents still ruled my world unless I left school and got a job to support them and myself for as long as I lived. There was no haste in me. My fascinating maturing body and brain began a slow and confusing yet exciting process, morphing me from a shy, insecure and emotionally battered adolescent into a socially inept and studious teenager. Bashed and bullied by an unforgiving society, they all sat back and expected me to flourish among clouds of hateful words and taunts.

Back at school and during the last few weeks of 1981, my classmates and I focused on our final exam. Our basic skills of reading, counting, and writing were topped up with general doses of historical, geographical, biological and scientific facts and data to store for a future reference, conversation or job. They taught boys some basic woodwork and the girls a bit of sewing and cooking. Assured of a passing grade, I also wanted to be one of the top ten pupils in class, if not school. Wishing everyone good luck, we put pens and pencil to paper, prayed and hoped for the best.

After the final paper, I was relieved yet anxious. It was never nice leaving friends and classmates behind. Our papers were marked, and school registers updated to track our grades and progress in case of lost report cards or for relocation purposes. The best or good news was that I passed, along with many of my classmates. The forty-five minutes or so walk to St Johns Road school would be something of the past. Our new school was closer and once the excitement died down, we got the usual lecture before starting our holidays. Reminded of the tougher road ahead, we had to work harder, impress all the new teachers. and the four years would be over before we knew it. Walking out of the gates for the last time, we raced home to share and spread the good news. Parents and relatives reiterated what our teachers had said: hard work awaited us. In hindsight it was funny that those who had never been to high school told you how difficult or tough it was, yet we never questioned their authority on the subject.

There was more good news when they told us about a special prize giving night that was to be held. The best pupils of 1981 at St John's Primary School would get certificates. This was a first for us from the poor side of town. Expecting no prizes, we had to be there, and were told to bring anyone and everyone to fill the seats. Kids who studied hard were to be recognized, hoping to encourage others to imitate and follow. We all expected the academic war between the Afrikaans and English-speaking kids, and the unspoken yet subtle fight between rich and poor hovered in the air. I walked into the Parkside Hall, minus my parents and siblings yet again, joining excited teachers and parents. The set of usual drunken uninvited guests made an appearance and a beeline for the food and juices laid out along the wall. The night commenced, and everyone clapped and whistled as expected. The bright kids walked confidently and proudly to collect their prizes, waving to the audience, family and friends. Lost among the many faces, everything blurred as I tried to blend in and relax. Caught up in the excitement, I never heard them announce the final prize of the night and neither did I hear them call my name out loud, missing my very first time in the spotlight. I felt hands pull at me, saw everyone stare at me as I was pushed out of my chair. Loud clapping and cheering followed as I numbly climbed the stairs, not at all sure what was happening.

Someone smiled at me, pushed a rolled-up piece of paper into my one hand and shook the other. My face and body felt hot, and I never heard a single word while on stage. I had no idea what to do but wait for a signal to go back to my seat. I turned to walk off the stage, praying I would not fall since my legs were shaking so badly. Blurry-eyed and heart racing, I staggered off to another round of applause and whistles. Hobbling past jutting feet and knees, while avoiding the hands trying to grab the paper in my hand, I heard the non-complimentary comments, my face getting hotter with shame. An adult voice reprimanded the culprit. Eventually someone unrolled the paper in my hand and unfolded it, eager to see what was written on it. It said I was the third best pupil of the year for 1981.

That a poor kid beat many others for a prize was a shock to just about everyone in my class, including myself. Those lonely nights hunched over candles and lamps paid off, and while hazy memories of that night remain, the writing on the certificate faded and sadly, it got lost or misplaced and no photographic evidence exists. Needless to say. I was proud as punch, yet my parents, relatives and siblings were not there to share my special moment – a pattern I encouraged for the rest of my life, intent to stand alone in my shame, and in glory.

My new-found fame as a mini-celebrity added an extra spring in my step and I milked the moment for every drop and penny. Praised for passing and winning a prize, it was feared I might join my brother and get suspended or drop out of school. That was never going to happen. Emotionally a child, yet physically an adult, I looked forward to the new chapter and challenge in my life, the much shorter school route a blessing. Sadly, there were the thugs and weather conditions we still had to face. The next four years a certainty, I took stock of things around me.

My siblings aged 17 and 20 respectively, still lived with my parents and me in the small shack, and my sister was the first one to step out of line. Coming home after her shifts, she disappeared for most of the evening, coming home later and later, and then not at all. Offering some lame excuse, her behaviour upset my parents, especially our mum, who fretted constantly. Rosie was a young single girl with no boyfriend that we knew of, so sleeping out was not the socially accepted thing at the time. People spread news or rumours and dragged your name into the gutters. The shack was a small place, so the smell of alcohol was hard to hide. Since no one drank any alcohol, my poor sister had a tough time, but she tried. Reprimanded for drinking and perhaps disgracing herself, my sister decided it was best to stay out the entire weekend to face my mother after the fun. She had no idea that her mother kept a vigil at the window, a ball of nerves and worry, jumping out of bed at the slightest sound, hoping to see her daughter come home to sleep, and we were kept from a good night's rest.

With no word about her whereabouts or well-being, we went looking for her, coming home alone, with little or no information. My mother made unexpected visits without raising any alarm, upset and worried her eldest child was becoming a handful. After a few days, my sister came home, contrite and ashamed, kept a low profile and behaved long enough to appease everyone. Her good behaviour short-lived, the cycle was duly repeated. We had no idea where she went, what she did or the people she partied with over the weekend. She never gave any explanation either. We knew she drank alcohol but had no idea how much she drank and if her friends looked after each other. Those hangover days crept in and she began to miss work, sending my mother into panic in case she got dismissed. We needed her small income, and since there was no chance to rest in the shack, my mother hounded and fussed until she was forced to go to work or get away and stay with friends and miss work either way. The smaller salary gave her away but if she went to work, it was fine.

Rosie was wise enough not to come home drunk. My father let his wife do her best to try and rein my sister in, while he watched her silently. I had no idea her antics were a topic of conversation in some homes, among friends and relatives. No one came out to tell us where she was, or warn us what was going on, except to watch her drink and party with people who did not have her best interests at heart. My lovely sister had at one time entered many local beauty pageants over weekends, before the lure of parties and drinking took centre stage.

My disobedient sister, coupled with my mother's constant nightly vigils, added to our disturbed sleeping pattern. I was not a parent, so never understood why she did not let Rosie stay out whenever she wanted. As a brother with a distorted emotional relation, I often snapped in annoyance and perhaps from lack of sleep. On the flip side, Frank came home, irrespective of the time. We had to leave the latch off the door, which bothered my mother who shopped at every sound. Either way, our sleep patterns were a mess, a snoring and coughing father adding to the equation. I was the well-behaved one of the lot.

Well, I had my childish moments of rebellion, which were short-lived when there was mention of a belt or a raised voice and stern look. I knew my place very well, and do I recall any beatings? Yes, I do. When we moved to East London, I was never given a hiding – the shack was too small. In Durban we had a bigger shack and then a proper house. One got dragged into the bedroom, beaten as you begged to behave. Someone might come in to stop or save you, but there was always a good enough beating to hit some manners and sense into you, until the next time.

overall, my parents were not the aggressive type, so we had a peaceful home life until my siblings spread their wings. I focused on baiting the boys, while it intensified the bashing meted out by the bullies. Shunned or shoved aside for my peculiar mannerisms, my inner sense of sadness and loneliness increased as I grew older, presenting a sociable facade in public as I sought out those less likely to hurt or ridicule me. Kids my own age intimidated me, the boys often misunderstood or misinterpreted my nature, while girls were suspicious of me in their midst. Drawn to smaller kids and older people, I found an innocent acceptance as I entertained and amused them with my queerness. Using every tool to flaunt the real me, they laughed and smiled at and with me, something very few people did for me.

The next four academic years of high school awaited us as my friends and I prepared to tackle them, some to prove a point and others to make their parents proud. I said I lacked the inner drive or urge to succeed, yet I was buoyed by a quiet assurance that I could get to the finishing line. Everyone treated me like the child I was, as we watched kids our age joins the adult world sooner than expected, by choice or circumstance. Feeling slightly off kilter, I expected someone or something to stop me as I was about to step into new and uncharted territory. I would not be alone; I had my classmates who might feel the same way, except I was the queer and odd one out. My older brother gave up his spot in high school, so it was my turn to have a go at it. No doubt everyone took a glance in my direction. My school friends expected it, my family and relatives waited and watched my progress diligently, and the amount of the paycheck that was eventually expected would rise with every passing school year.

John Bisseker Senior Secondary School would be my third school since relocating to East London. My parents had some idea where I spent most of the day, while many school friends were clueless about where I settled in at night. Or, I innocently thought they did. I had no idea the shack dwellers, including my parents, begged to be moved into a real house, so I never saw the disappointed faces after each letter denied them a chance of a better living environment. They were told to be patient. I was fourteen and I had stepped into the shack as an eight-year-old, only to find myself still sleeping on a single bed, next to my dad's feet. From primary school kid to a teenage high school student, I desperately needed some privacy, even though I had no idea it was owed to me.

David, the boy kissed and fondled by friends, had grown into George, a gay teenager, bullied and ostracized for allowing boys to grope and treat him like a girl. Teased and mocked about it, no one tackled the topic to understand how I felt or try to soothe my confused feelings and mixed emotions. I knew what I was, they hated me for it, so we had to live with or around the issue. My attraction to another boy would never go away, nor was I ever going to change how I felt deep inside. The past seven years I had been treated like a girl, made to think, act, feel and behave like one. We may debate why and how it had come to this. Was Harvey the catalyst or was it meant to be? Shy and self-conscious, introverted and so insecure, I wore a heavy silent cloak to mask a layer of self-doubt, low self-esteem and misery. Good at hiding my happy and funny soul, I craved to escape and finally be accepted.

Resigning myself to the accustomed pattern of my daily experiences, my high school years were destined to be no different. Physically fit and healthy yet burdened by the psychological scars and a dented psyche, it was time to move forward. My new high school, like most of them, had a Latin motto, Facta Non Verba, translating to Deeds Not Words.

Educational institutions chose a motto derived from the language of law, scholars and the church, conveying a sense of worldliness and sophistication. None of the teachers, nor my friends and I envisioned the accuracy of the Latin proverb when we stepped through the gates of John Bisseker Senior Secondary School in 1982. The best was yet to come.

Chapter 34: sadly, there is none, but this is not the end

I do promise an exciting second instalment is on the way. Thank you very much for reading. May I mention, names have been changed to protect real characters. The spelling of mentioned places has changed in the new South Africa, so kindly excuse the original names used in this copy. I want to apologize for my own spelling or grammatical errors. I hope they do not distract from the story. My idea was to give the book personal feel, imagine I am telling you the story face to face. Feel free to leave a review or comment on Amazon or my Facebook page.

Love, Peace, Strength and Happiness

Georgie

Ps; A very special mention to some wonderful people who have travelled the past four years, and many more, with me. If I have forgotten a name, please forgive me, but there are two books on the way, unless I have a nervous breakdown before editing the manuscripts. So, in random order, here we go;

Ashley Johnson, Denver Adams, Gerhard Grimett, Jon Plowman, Laurelle Hughes Carre, Tanya Casoojee, Liz Sunker, Jonathan Adams, Emily Mkuchane, Genoulda Moore, Penny Marais, Ingrid Petersen -Anyakudo, Devine Lottering, Caroline Davidson-Makgabo, Gerald Bedeker and family, Liesl Wehncke and Angela Blake

Andre Pretorius, Michelle Alwar-Slijepcevic and family, Simpi Skosana, Noel Maholwana, Trevor, Winniefred, Jana and JJ Fourie, Dawn Fraser, The Ajham family; Ben, Toni, Ashley and Jessie, Rory and Melanie Holtman, Jacqueline

Voget, Jerenice Stafford Goosen and Stanley and Debbie Holtman.

Candice Pennington and family, Lucy Pennington- Jackson, Jamie Nortje, Lorraine Richards, Kingsley Hutchinson, Isam Karim, Yolanda Jones, Andre, Venesia, Gabby and Alicia Paries, Tessa Richards and members of The Sedibeng Kzn Bookclub, Shereen, Rholene, Eugene, Lenise Llewellyn and Jamiellah Llewellyn Domingo.

Lynn Peters, Jennifer Roberts, Maynard Kraak, David Phillis, Virginia and Sedikah Doanns, Lavinia Cooper and family, Germaine Halliburton, Ingrid Bosch, Rochelle Kleinhans, Mariann Mckay, Darian, Cheslyn, Johan and Felicia Nys.

Eleanor Johnson, Jenny Crickmore-Thompson, Anthony Noble, Nicola Scott, Judy Hargreaves, Ursula Revada Gaitskill and Edith Wynne-Trollip. A special thank you to all colleagues in South Africa and United Kingdom, past and present for putting up with my madness. Love you all for the wonderful support.

Thank you to Andre Rangasamy for photograph on the back cover.

Finally, to the three very special young ladies in my life, Ludmilla, Lana and Lauren, your uncle loves you all very much. Caleb, Haylin and Keano, my two tinier nephews and little niece, may your future be bright and beautiful.

Thank you, guys, for keeping me entertained and waiting patiently for this very first instalment. To all readers, you are simply the best and hope you enjoyed my first attempt at writing.

Love from me, Georgie

Printed in Great Britain
by Amazon